THE FALL
OF THE
ASSADS

The End of Half a Century of Tyranny in Syria
and Its Impact on the West

James Snell

GIBSON SQUARE

For Ray and Monica Snell

Published for the first time by Gibson Square in 2025

UK   Tel: +44 (0)20 7096 1100
US   Tel: +1 646 216 9813

info@gibsonsquare.com
gibsonsquare.com

Papers used by Gibson Square are natural, recyclable products made from wood grown in sustainable forests; inks used are vegetable based. Manufacturing conforms to ISO 14001, and is accredited to FSC and PEFC chain of custody schemes. Colour-printing is through a certified CarbonNeutral® company that offsets its CO2 emissions.

CONTENTS

ACKNOWLEDGEMENTS

This pale work only exists because of the work of many others—editors, sources, colleagues and friends and family—who have tried to give my reporting shape and factual integrity. I must refer most notably to all the people I have interviewed over the years, on the record and off, for every outlet under the sun. Their thoughts have shaped the book, though it is all my words and my fault.

Special thanks to Elizabeth Tsurkov, who the whole world wants to see freed; and Gareth Browne, Suhail al-Ghazi, Rasha al-Aqeedi, Hanin Ghaddar, Mamoon Alabbasi, Iman Zayat, Haid Haid, Simon Speakman Cordall, Katy Stone, James Robins, Sheeffah Shiraz, Bente Scheller, Rashad Ali, Charlie Hoyle, Hamish de Bretton-Gordon, Michael Pregent, Hassan Hassan, Michael Weiss, Oz Katerji, Anjuli R. K. Shere, Phillip Smyth, James Robins, David Patrikarakos, Azeem Ibrahim OBE, James Palmer, Caroline Rose, Faysal Itani, my former colleagues at the New Lines Institute; and many, many others unnamed for security or good taste or both. And greatest thanks and humble obeisance to the profoundly dedicated group of people who read the manuscript and corrected, between them, so much: my parents, Dominic Snell and Melanie Snell; and dear friends, Mia Rocquemore, Alex Rowell, and Kyle Orton. It's all thanks to you.

INTRODUCTION

When Bashar al-Assad, the hereditary dictator of Syria, fled Damascus in early December 2024, he left a country in ruins. Syria's cities, newly conquered by rebel forces, were shadows of what they had been fifteen years before. Whole neighbourhoods were destroyed, districts flattened by bombing and shelling and condemned by the bulldozer. Many towns that had been depopulated by the fighting were annihilated and left abandoned. They littered the country.

Maybe a million had died in the thirteen-year-long war that Assad had launched on the people of Syria. He began the war when they demonstrated for government reforms in early 2011, and his security forces responded with bullets. When the people of Syria demanded an end to the death camps and the torture chambers. When the state replied by filling both until they were so full of bodies there was no air left to breathe.

Assad is one of this century's great monsters. He will be justly reviled. It is still possible he will see the inside of a court—Syria's government was bureaucratic to a fault. It kept good records of the crimes of Assad and his men. They fill warehouses, and the warehouses of paper, of evidence, are growing across the world. Assad has fled to Russia, but the threat of trial ought to follow him until his dying day. Many Syrians are happier than words can express that their country has been liberated. Those rejoicing all agree: there is no chance of Assad returning to power. For the first time in fifty years, no one from the House of Assad rules Syria. The rule of that evil family is over.

This book traces the degeneration of Syria's state and government—from a tyranny where the walls had ears and the intelligence agencies claimed to see all—into a slaughterhouse beyond twenty-first century comparison. It shows that a war which began as a bid by Assad to hold onto power became instead a war of total destruction: either the whole of Syria would be liquidated, reduced to the quiet of the graveyard, or the regime itself would succumb.

Syria fractured and fragmented over the course of the war, with no side of this multi-stranded civil conflict able to conquer the others. All until the Assad regime fell as a result of its own corruption and internal contradictions, its failures of state capacity, its international drug trafficking, to an offensive beginning in late November 2024. The whole rotten edifice imploded around Assad, coming crashing down once the door was kicked in.

The collapse of the Assad regime was so sudden that few predicted it.

What began as one rebel offensive in the country's distant north reached Damascus within two weeks. The future of Syria remains uncertain. How will the former leaders of Hayat Tahrir al-Sham, the Islamist group (now formally dissolved) which began that cascading series of offensives, govern the country—in alliance with fellow rebel groups, keeping peace with the Kurdish-dominated autonomous areas in Syria's north-east? Or might the country fracture again into warring parts?

This book is the result of almost fourteen years' study of Syria's protests and civil war, and reporting done for innumerable newspapers and magazines. It is the product of an author who has seen many things die in Syria: friends, sources, cities, political parties, radio stations, social organisations—but who is still hopeful for the future of the country.

I did not expect to see Syria free of the regime of the Assads in my lifetime, and yet now it is. Syrians have survived civil war and displacement, the loss of their homes and families, the seeming destruction of every dream they had—and the survival, for longer than any could have feared, of a system of savagery and barbarism that, now it is being revealed to the wider world, is so terrible it is difficult to believe it ever existed.

They have survived all of this, and now their country is free. The future is unknown. But all agree: there is no going back. The Assad regime has forever fallen. The regime said that Assad and his regime would rule forever. Across Syria, late last year, a new slogan was chanted. Forever is over. Syria is free.

PART ONE

KINGDOM OF FEAR

'The people want the fall of the regime!'
Arab Spring revolutionary slogan

'Assad or we burn the country.'
Regime slogan

2

THE GIRAFFE

The twenty-first century's most evil tyrant was never meant to rule his country. Bashar was the second son of Syria's dictator, Hafez al-Assad. As a second son, Bashar was not destined for greatness. He trained as a doctor in Syria and practised briefly in army medicine. In the 1990s, he was packed off to London to train as an ophthalmologist. While his father ruled Syria, Bashar al-Assad was an ophthalmologist in Britain. If you had eye surgery in London thirty years ago, it's possible he was your doctor.

Some people still remember, or claim to remember, Bashar al-Assad from those days. They called him unremarkable, not someone who stood out—rather like the things people say of serial killers, after the fact. He kept himself to himself; always well-mannered. But the thing that marked Assad out was his parentage. His father, Hafez al-Assad, was Syria's military tyrant. He had been in power since 1970. Bashar's father had a wide face, a large forehead, thin white hair and a wide jaw.

Hafez al-Assad had once been an air force pilot who had left a background of rural poverty. He was fired with resentment—he hated the rich of both town and countryside. An ardent Arab nationalist, Hafez joined the Ba'ath Party in his youth, but he became disillusioned with the party's civilian leaders. Quietly and with the conspiratorial aspect that defined Assadist politics, Hafez formed his own cell of young officers. They carried out a coup in 1963, toppling what was, for a time, a semi-democracy in Syria.

In the seven years that followed, Hafez al-Assad weaved and conspired and picked off his rivals one by one until finally, by 1970, he alone held supreme power as Syria's president. Hafez was a man of history in a way his son Bashar never was: a wannabe bodybuilder in his youth (there are pictures to prove it), Hafez became a real strongman in politics: cunning, devious, capable of planning and deliberation but also deep irrational hatred—including of Syria's Sunni majority—which culminated in great explosions of violence.

In 1982, twelve years after Hafez took office, a test of his will to power came along. Demonstrations turned into an attempt at a religious revolution in the Syrian city of Hama. Over four weeks, the army and air force of Hafez al-Assad first levelled and then stormed the city.

Tens of thousands of civilians were killed in the fighting. The exact number of dead is hard to know; estimates range between 20,000 and 40,000.

Many thousands more opponents of the regime disappeared into prisons from which they never emerged. One man, Raghad al-Tatary, an air force pilot who refused orders to bomb Hama, was only released from prison in December 2024. By 1994, Hafez al-Assad had been dictator for twenty-four years.

Other opponents of Hafez were not religious fundamentalists. But they were no better treated than the religious men. Communists and leftists like Yassin al-Haj Saleh (imprisoned by the Hafez regime from 1980 to 1996) and Riad al-Turk (imprisoned four times, repeatedly tortured, and held in solitary confinement for almost eighteen years after 1980) spent much of their lives behind bars. Both of those men practised wholly nonviolent activism. Riad al-Turk was known at the time of his death on the first day of 2024, the year of Syria's liberation from Bashar, as the Old Man of the Syrian opposition. He had earlier been called Syria's Mandela.

Even in death, Hafez loomed over the shoulder of his son Bashar. Statues of him dotted the country, and his image stared down from posters, murals, and mosaics across the land. He was a demonic presence for Syria's revolutionaries. Even though he'd been dead for 11 years by 2011, the protesters still chanted against him (one of the most common was 'Curse your soul, Hafez!'). And fourteen years later, when Bashar's regime fell, Syrians rushed to torch Hafez's opulent tomb in Latakia and topple all of Hafez's statues. This was the father of the London eye doctor who kept himself to himself and did not strike anyone as all that remarkable.

Possibly Bashar al-Assad was content to operate in London and to enjoy whatever stolen wealth and status his father's position afforded him. He might have remained in London to this day. But this is not what happened. It was the death of Bashar al-Assad's brother, Bassel, in a high-speed car crash in 1994 (Bassel was driving to the airport at over 100 miles per hour without a seatbelt and hit a barrier) that made Bashar Syria's heir apparent. It turned a man who had previously been described as a 'geek' and unassuming into the inheritor of the throne of his military dictator father.

The wheels of tyranny move quickly. Bassel al-Assad, the former heir, had been lionised from his earliest days as the ideal Syrian youth: a champion athlete and equestrian. Bassel was in reality a hairy man who looked tired, older than his years, in photographs. But now Bassel was dead, and it was the turn of Bashar to be elevated to the anteroom of supreme power. Soon pictures of Bashar began to appear alongside his father and late brother in the propaganda posters that, until the regime's fall in late 2024, dotted the government-held parts of Syria. For over fifty years, the image of the two Assads, father and son, stared down at Syria's people. In 1994, Bashar al-Assad was not quite thirty. He was tall and thin, with a long neck and large ears. He had a weak chin. We do not know at what time people started to nickname him Zarafa, 'the Giraffe'.

The next few years sped by for Assad. He was conducted through Syria's military and political societies by an array of brigadiers and intelligence officers. He was handed a shiny military rank, and time commanding prestigious units, to give him some status among soldiers. And all the while, the propaganda of his father filtered down, telling the public that Bashar al-Assad was the guardian of the state, the hope for the future, a man who would rule Syria for many decades after his father's time in power came to an end. As Hafez al-Assad aged and began to struggle, his son was inducted into the attractions of absolute power.

Hafez al-Assad died of a heart attack on June 10, 2000. After some phoney deliberations, his son Bashar was elected to take his father's place as president. Hafez al-Assad had built a state of mass surveillance that was tightly managed through institutions controlled by the ruling Ba'ath party and its allies. All politics that did not go through the party was illegitimate. Speaking freely risked ending up in one of the regime's dread prisons, risked torture, risked death. Minority languages like Kurdish were heavily restricted. It was illegal under the Assad regime for Kurdish children to be taught in their native language. The Assads were Alawites, part of a sect related to Shia Islam, with its historic roots in the coastal Latakia governorate. For those who were not Alawites, it was hard to get good marks at school, to be selected for the best universities, and to get senior government or army jobs. A small minority lorded it over the rest of Syria. And at the top of that minority was the Assad family.

This was the state that Bashar al-Assad inherited when he became president on July 17, 2000. He won a fake presidential election a week earlier, in which he was the only candidate. The government said Assad had won over 99 per cent of the vote. Many hoped, without evidence, that the dictator's young son (Bashar al-Assad was thirty-four in mid-2000) would not follow the blood-drenched path of his father. Hafez al-Assad had been a monster. He had invaded Lebanon in 1976, with Syrian troops still occupying the country in 2000. In Lebanon, Hafez had mounted a campaign of terrorism and assassination to destroy his rivals. At home, he was the centre of a Stalinist personality cult which described Hafez as an almost divine being, the country's 'Eternal Leader'.

The world used every excuse to pretend the new president might be a better man than Hafez. Amnesty International welcomed the announced release of 600 political prisoners in November 2000, despite noting that over 1,500 'prisoners of conscience' still remained behind bars. France gave Assad the Legion of Honour in 2001. The Damascus Spring, a brief but intense period of intellectual discussion in Syria between 2000 and 2001, was subsequently clamped down upon heavily by the government. But few outside the country noticed or cared.

Assad would be a moderating influence on the country's generals, some wrote with no evidence. He would make Syria a twenty-first-century nation, a land with the values of email and satellite TV, rather than the values of the dark ages. That's what some said, with no reason behind them. Peter Mandelson, then a washed-up former minister, wrote in the *Independent* in November 2001 that Assad was 'an intelligent and cultured individual' whose solemn 'task is to create enlightenment and spread reform without providing a pretext for rabble-rousers and religious reactionaries to stir the masses and pitch them against his rule'.

When Bashar al-Assad married a woman of Syrian origin and British birth called Asma, much of the world gushed and swooned at her beauty. This swooning did not stop for eleven years. Asma was given the glossy magazine treatment by *Vogue* as late as February 2011, in a piece calling her a 'rose in the desert'. Asma al-Assad, *Vogue* panted, was 'glamorous, young, and very chic—the freshest and most magnetic of first ladies'. She was 'a thin, long-limbed beauty with a trained analytic mind who dresses with cunning understatement', Joan Juliet Buck wrote, her household was managed on 'wildly democratic principles'. The elegant president's wife who stirred fondue while *Vogue* had fits ended up a Lady Macbeth to her husband's cruel regime.

The couple may have thought of themselves as reformers, but they were reformers who did not reform. While Asma al-Assad was first lady, the prisons were ever full of her husband's political opponents. The torture chambers saw their regular quotas of victims. Murder was the sustaining element of the regime. And Asma breathed not a public word of restraint, never issued the smallest rebuke, never indicated her own disquiet with the killings and the mass surveillance of the society in which she lived. Seeing the ten-foot-high posters of her husband, venerated as a living god by the state, on every building or wall large enough to hold them—all of that seemed natural to her.

Her husband the president, who told *Vogue* he studied eye surgery 'because it's very precise, it's almost never an emergency, and there is very little blood', never modernised his country, never led a good government, never improved lives in Syria. Instead, he headed a regime which washed all of Syria and its neighbours in a great tide of blood, a tide which has not receded for thirteen terrible years.

They lived in a presidential palace in Damascus that was so filled with beautiful and expensive things that it took some time, when the regime fell, to be looted. When Assad fled Syria in 2024, the palace was emptied of Asma's pretty dresses, all of them expensive, and things like embroidered chairs and curtains. Burly bearded men carried dresses wrapped in plastic and tissue paper out of the front doors of the palaces. Who knows whether they intended to give the dresses to their wives, or to sell them on a market that may now see a glut of taffeta and silk.

New people wandered the corridors of more than one palace. In another of them, high in the hills above Damascus, they found a fully equipped gym and two hot tubs, separated by a few feet. One is never enough for a dictator and his family. Nearby, in the presidential garage, curious reporters were shown dozens of cars of different makes and models, all for the use of one family and their staff, in a country where millions died in a civil war, and the minimum wage is about $12.50 per month.

The family photo albums were not taken to Russia when the dictator and his family fled to Moscow. They were poured over with some interest. Many of the pictures showed Assad posing in his underwear, or in speedos in swimming pools. There were so many of those pictures that Syrians started referring to Assad not as the Giraffe, but as Abu Kalsun, the 'Father of the Underwear'.

These palaces were within a short drive, almost within sight, of the prisons filled and the torture chambers busy. Within sight of the mass graves now being discovered, their horrors unearthed. A photograph of Assad blacked up, in fancy dress, at a party. Not far from the prisons, not far from the mass graves.

2

BEFORE THE WAR, A WAR

For dictators, terrorism always has its uses. The attacks of September 11, 2001, were among the best things that ever happened to Bashar al-Assad. On that day, jihadist terrorists from the al-Qaeda network flew airliners into buildings, striking at the heart of the United States in attacks that killed 2,996 people and disfigured the New York skyline. In one morning, for Assad, the past was forgotten—the slate wiped clean. Assad, like many of his neighbours, fell over himself to condemn the attacks on America. Assad's allies in Hezbollah, a Lebanese political party and militia, had committed acts of terrorism across the world, including the murder of hundreds of Americans. But luckily for Assad, 9/11 was the fault of someone else. The United States was in shock, and reacted with snap decisiveness to the attack it had suffered. Within a week, Afghanistan and its Taliban government were in America's sights. That is where Osama bin Laden, leader of al-Qaeda, had his bases and his training camps. That is where the United States would fight first.

Syria could watch and wait. Assad could duck and cover. Very soon, Iraq, governed by Saddam Hussein, was also under American suspicion. Iraq was accused by America of developing a nuclear weapons programme, and of being an ally and helper of bin Laden and al-Qaeda. For Assad, this was a tricky situation. The governments of Iraq and Syria had long hated each other, but now the two were getting closer. Syria and Iraq shared some financial ties. Smuggling between the two countries was very profitable. But Saddam had been a great rival of Assad's father. Syria had fought against Iraq as part of the world coalition in the 1991 Gulf War. Iraq was an enemy, and it would, in theory, be good for Assad to see his enemy weakened.

Since Bashar al-Assad had come to power, his government had also grown increasingly close to Iran, which was the greatest enemy of Saddam. Iran and Iraq had fought a very bloody war from 1980 to 1988. Iran was the sponsor and backer of Hezbollah, which together with Syria dominated and occupied Lebanon. Inside Syria, the regime portrayed the upcoming invasion of Iraq as a Jewish-American plot to destroy the Muslim world. Assad opposed the Iraq invasion publicly, too. But to the Americans, however, Assad said that he was a sensible man, a man they could do business with—unlike that lunatic tyrant Saddam. 'I am not Saddam Hussein', Assad told *Time* magazine in 2005. 'I want to co-operate'.

To the Arab and Muslim world, Assad wanted to be a hero standing up for their interests against the Americans. But to the Americans, Assad wanted to be useful. This was a tall order, given the long list of problems the United States had with Syria: its links to terrorism, money laundering, international organised crime and more.

But the media machine worked itself into gear regardless. This was a great change in both Syria's and Assad's personal PR. Most people outside the region did not know much about Syria. September 11 was a good time for the regime to tell outsiders its version of events. Syria was a backward place, regime agents said, but its fine young president was trying to change that. Go into villages outside the capital, they said, and you will see old women wearing the veil. In Damascus, there are nightclubs and the businessmen all wear suits while their wives spend money in expensive shops without covering their faces. And the energy and water systems in the rural areas are a scandal. But don't worry about that. Something is going to be done in due course. And don't think about the torture chambers either. They are filled only with bad people, the kinds of people you wouldn't like to live in your country.

Assad was able to launder his reputation quite effectively in this way. It is at this time that the international press first started to refer to Syria, a society run by a small ethnic group whose leaders were adherents of a small religious group, as a secular society under threat from a combination of the majority, who were Sunni Arabs, and a smaller and more hardcore group of hardline jihadists, the sort of men who flew airliners into the World Trade Center.

Assad's Syria was more than willing to share its torture chambers with foreigners if it helped the state and the president. It was good to do America favours as the War on Terror grew. Syria was a happy participant in what the CIA and American authorities called 'extraordinary rendition', where suspects linked with terrorism were sent to foreign countries to be roughed up on America's behalf. Maher Arar, a Canadian with Syrian citizenship, was deported by American authorities to Syria in 2002, where he was viciously tortured by the agents of the Assad regime. Eventually, years later, he was given huge compensation by the Canadian government and an official apology. Arar was not alone.

Investigations by journalists including the *New Yorker*'s Jane Mayer found that Syria was one of the 'most common' destinations for terror suspects that the United States wanted interrogated. In Syria's case, interrogation always means torture. But torture does not work. It is not good at producing useful intelligence. And the Assad regime's torturers never proved their worth. Those suspects tortured in Syria at America's behest ought to have been interrogated by the United States under its own laws, rather than handed off to an avid but incompetent state, Syria, which tortured not for information but because its intelligence services knew how to do nothing else.

All this useful torture strangely changed how Assad and his country were seen in America. Syria was no longer just a repressive tyranny which exported terrorism to its neighbours and occupied Lebanon (the Bush administration acknowledged that by motions in Congress and a UN Security Council resolution in 2004). Instead, Syria and its president were each allies in the new wars on terrorism and 'instability'. Some of Assad's domestic opponents were conservative Islamists from the Sunni branch of Islam. This was enough for many American and world leaders: al-Qaeda, the perpetrators of the 9/11 attacks, were also Sunni Muslims. Therefore, to some deluded people in Washington and around the world, the people Assad and his father had locked up and tortured were automatically the same as al-Qaeda. To many desperate and foolish people in the West, Assad was now a partner in the global War on Terror.

But ordinary Syrians resented being ruled by a tyrant. They showed it in many small ways. In 2004, violence broke out in the northern town of Qamishli during a football match. Guns were fired into the crowd by the authorities. The local population, mostly Kurds, responded to this violence by holding public protests, and vandalising some regime symbols in their neighbourhood. The response was violent and out of all proportion. The Assad regime sent in tanks, helicopters, and hundreds of soldiers.

They fired indiscriminately on Kurdish protesters, killing 36 and wounding at least 160. The crackdown continued and morphed into more general terrorising of the local population: at least 2,000 people, mostly Kurds, were arrested. Soon after, the regime banned all unapproved Kurdish political parties. From then on, Syria's Kurds would not have a legal voice.

This is what the Assad regime did. When it was not torturing to order, its intelligence agencies and army were cracking down on ethnic minorities and people who wanted reform, killing as many as possible and disappearing the rest. Syria under Bashar al-Assad was a kingdom of fear, a place where saying the wrong word to anyone might mean arrest, torture and death. The Mukhabarat (intelligence agencies) could be anywhere. Their informants could be anyone. Some people did not tell their own families what they thought, either because they feared being informed on themselves, or because they did not want their families to know anything incriminating if they were picked up by authorities.

People close to the regime were able to live lavishly, to attract and spend great wealth. They got government contracts and jobs; their children went to the best schools and universities. They could become rich and live something of the good life. But the majority of Syria's population was politically powerless, living in near poverty, and worried that the wrong word said to the wrong person would mean arrest and death or torture.

The War on Terror gave Assad a lifeline. But it was a lifeline with a time limit. He could not remain in power just because the Americans gave him people to torture in his prisons. If Assad had used the first decade of his time as president to make political compromises, even to make the economy work better and less corruptly, he might have had a chance to retain power. But he did neither of those things. He never compromised with anyone. The prisons remained full and the executioners busy. He never tried to make Syria a prosperous place for people who weren't Ba'ath party members, who weren't connected by race or family or religion to the president. For a decade, the population who had suffered thirty years of dictatorship under the president's father saw the young leader age into a complacent autocrat, changing nothing, giving them nothing, wishing only to remain in power—to stay in power personally, to keep power and wealth in the hands of his family and party. Assad's regime did not know how to do anything else. Something had to give.

3

THE SHOCK OF THE NEW

By 2011, Saddam Hussein had been overthrown and put on trial and executed. Colonel Muammar Gaddafi, president of Libya, had announced his intention to give up his nuclear weapons programme. In Afghanistan and Iraq, victorious wars against the Taliban and Saddam Hussein's government had bogged down, with international forces and the new governments of those countries fighting militant groups which increasingly recruited and drew their financing from overseas. Bashar al-Assad was one of the great helpers of the terrorist insurgencies in Iraq.

From 2003, while his government was torturing people at the behest of the American CIA, Assad started to encourage Syrians to travel to Iraq to fight the Americans and the new Iraqi government. Some of the stories connected to this are amusing. One of them is that the bus depot where the jihadists first embarked on their journey to eastern Syria, from where they would cross the border into Iraq to fight, was not far from the American embassy in Damascus. Another is that one of these young men, sent by Assad to Iraq, fought under the name of Abu Mohammad al-Jolani. That man, born in Saudi Arabia but of Syrian origin and upbringing, returned to fight in his home country after 2011 and was instrumental in Assad's overthrow in November and December 2024 as the leader of Hayat Tahrir al-Sham. He is now the interim president of Syria.

Many of the fighters who would defeat Assad in 2024 grew up in Syria in the post-9/11 period. They remember it as a time of profound anxiety and notable repression. A war was being fought next door. The government wanted them scared. Al-Qaeda and the heirs of Saddam could surge over the border and cut your throats at night, people were told. Only the state keeps you safe, only the great leader protects you.

Daily life was still a struggle. Ordinary people were shaken down for cash by government employees and party members. People noticed that the government did not appear very good at cracking down on criminals, and focused its energy on them instead. Memoirs of Syrians who grew up in this time describe casual beatings by intelligence agency operatives and members of government-affiliated gangs. A growing sense of hopelessness pervaded the country. Where were the benefits of the new century? They had not arrived in Syria. In 2000, about four in ten of Syria's population were estimated to be under the age of fifteen. Ten years later, this generation was on the cusp of adulthood. What had Syria got to give them?

The country's economy was in constant crisis. As the population grew, the price of everything rose. Economic reforms would have meant political reforms: transparency, freer markets, and the rule of law. All of these things were impossible in a dictatorship like Syria's. When experts were appointed to grow the economy, they complained the intelligence agencies interfered with their work. Some of them quit. Others just did a bad job. As small pieces of modernisation took place, Syria actually grew more corrupt. It was an unfree society. People who were close to the government could take advantage of family and party ties. They flaunted their wealth more visibly and with less taste than ever before.

All of this angered many Syrians. Whatever the president said, Syria was not a free place and was not open for business. Housing was expensive, food was expensive. There were fewer and fewer jobs even as government salaries rose. Poverty for Syria's young population was the inevitable result.

Meanwhile, the machinery of terror continued working just fine. Syrian soldiers still occupied Lebanon. On 14 February 2005, the former prime minister of Lebanon, Rafic Hariri, was assassinated in a massive bombing in Beirut. No one has ever served time in prison for this murder. Subsequent investigations lay the blame at the foot of some combination of Syria and their allies in Hezbollah. The Special Tribunal for Lebanon did convict a Hezbollah member, Salim Ayyash, in absentia in 2020—but he has not seen the inside of a jail, and no one else has been touched by the hand of the law. This behaviour was outrageous, the product of a president or a state out of control. Daily protests began in Beirut demanding that someone who knew something give them 'the truth' about what had happened.

The murder of Hariri was a big miscalculation. Within a year, Syrian soldiers left Lebanon, forced out by unexpected public outcry. American pressure, against the Syrian occupation of Lebanon, which might have slackened thanks to the favours Assad did the CIA, intensified. In Lebanon, demonstration followed demonstration. What had been intended to show Assad's and Hezbollah's strength and impunity instead made them hated figures. The Assad regime's desire to kill its rivals and reckless willingness to use violence in relatively small disputes had blown up in its face. In the twenty years since, that happened again and again.

This ought to have been a warning sign. A sign that the Assad regime saw violence as a good tool to use against its enemies, and did not think much about the consequences of using force. Such a regime, headed by the president it had, was unlikely to moderate or reform itself without immense pressure from outside. If it could murder a foreign political leader with such carelessness, who knew what it would not stoop to do if it felt at risk? If it felt justified in doing anything to survive? But by and large, the world was busy elsewhere, and few people outside Lebanon cared all that much about the fate of that country's former prime minister. Not enough to trace his killing back to Damascus, to predict the violence that would erupt in Syria, the problem the Assad regime would present for the whole world.

In Syria itself, the economic crisis attracted some official attention. In the rest of the world, it went largely unnoticed. Across the Middle East and in North Africa, a generation of young people came of age in societies which were run by old men in military uniforms and clerical robes, who did not understand economics, and who could not promise them peace or justice or political liberty or the good life. They saw people in foreign countries on TV and their phones; they spoke to them through new social media apps. They could see that other people, only a few hundred miles away, got to lead normal lives without fear of the government putting them in prison for saying something critical of the president or Supreme Leader.

The beginning of the Arab Spring that arrived in late December 2010 was one long cascade, a tidal wave of protest that took military leaders, grey-suited dictators and religious officials by total surprise. It was a long shout of dissatisfaction at being offered fake elections contested by the same old candidates, of being beaten up and tortured by the police, of having no future to look forward to but more tyranny, more poverty, more failure.

First, Tunisia's dictator, Zine El Abidine Ben Ali, was ousted after less than a month of demonstrations (prompted by the fiery suicide of Mohamed Bouazizi, a market seller who had been extorted for a bribe he couldn't afford to pay by government officials, on 17 December 2010). By the end of January 2011—after security forces' firing on protesters did not stop the protests—Ben Ali had resigned and fled the country to Saudi Arabia. Demonstrations in Egypt against the thirty-year rule of Hosni Mubarak began on 25 January 2011. Protesters marched, they occupied Tahrir Square in central Cairo, and civil disobedience generally reigned. By 11 February 2011, Mubarak was gone. Protests in Morocco, Algeria, Oman, Yemen, Jordan, and Syria took place in January. Syria's true revolution, however, was not to begin until March, when it would be sparked by an act of such viciousness, such savagery, that it is still remembered almost one and a half decades later, after thirteen years of demonstrations and civil war, and innumerable other acts of violence which have come and gone across Syria's tragic path.

4

THE REVOLUTION OF DIGNITY

They were inspired by the protests which had emerged in Syria in January 2011, and the end of the dictatorships in Tunisia and Egypt. Some boys in Daraa, in Syria's south, painted revolutionary slogans on a wall at their school on February 16. The graffiti said 'it's your turn next, doctor', referring to Assad, the former London ophthalmologist. Naief Abazid, who was then fourteen, said later that he had painted the slogan. It didn't take long for him and his fellow boys to be discovered. Abazid was arrested by the regime and, in an act of shocking violence that was completely ordinary for its officials, he was tortured every day for weeks. Beaten, hung by his wrists from the ceiling, whipped with cords. He was forced into a small space and later thrown against a wall. He was kept in solitary confinement, at fourteen.

Abazid survived his ordeal and survived a shooting later, as well. Abazid was interviewed by a journalist in Vienna, years later. He got out of Syria. Abazid was tortured so that he would give up the names of his school friends. Those he named were also tortured until they gave up the names of others. Twenty-three of them were eventually in the custody of the Mukhabarat secret police. They disappeared into the hands of the state. When the boys' parents asked authorities about their children, and demanded them back, Atef Najib, the local commander of the secret police, told the boys' fathers to go home. They had lost their children, he is claimed to have said; it was their job now to make more. And if they could not do it, Najib is also alleged to have boasted, the men of Daraa could give their wives over to his fighters, who would do it for them.

Meanwhile, the boys were kept for over a month, tortured and beaten. The families of the boys organised demonstrations, calling on the regime to release their sons. Soon, news of the children spread across the country, where other demonstrations were already beginning. By mid-March, protests had started across Syria. March 15 was called the Day of Rage, as demonstrations broke out in Damascus and Aleppo, Syria's second largest city.

Organised online and by phone, protests seemed to the authorities watching to begin almost spontaneously. The authorities, with their secret police, their batons and water cannons, were outmatched. The thugs of the state, nicknamed shabiha ('ghosts'), alternately beat protesters or infiltrated them, but they could not stop the demonstrations. On March 18, more people took to the streets. It was called the Friday of Dignity, with protests in

Damascus, al-Hasakah, Daraa, Deir Ezzor, and Hama—all important provincial capitals. Already, the state showed its hand, with widespread violence and the killing of protesters. Less than a week later, an elite formation of the Syrian army, the Fourth Division, stormed a mosque in Daraa, killing some of the assembled.

On March 25, the funerals of those killed erupted into demonstrations, with tens of thousands taking part in other protests taking place nationwide. The violence was inevitable, with clashes reported in the international press, and many claimed to have been killed.

Some concessions were offered by the state: perhaps prisoners might be released, if everyone went home. But these were false promises, as soon said as seen through. On March 30, Bashar al-Assad gave a speech to the Syrian parliament, the People's Assembly. Assad joked his way through the address, and the members of parliament sycophantically laughed at his jokes. Outside the parliament, however, the violence was just beginning. It would not stop for almost fourteen years. Daraa itself was the cradle of the revolution. It was soon under siege as government thugs of all descriptions descended on the city.

Within weeks, it was clear the regime could not respond peacefully to these protests. Its efforts were all spent on the mechanisms of terror and intimidation. Every time demonstrators went out onto the streets, in whatever numbers they could muster, they risked being fired upon and arrested, they risked torture and death. And yet they still went out, day after day, in cities increasingly falling under siege, demanding freedom. The crowds swelled and grew, people flooded into the streets across Syria, pouring into ancient squares to reel and chant revolutionary slogans. Demonstrations in Daraa were said to have numbered a hundred thousand.

A pattern soon set in. Protests would begin and grow, with thousands on the streets. The local forces of the regime—police, army, secret police, paramilitaries—would fire into the crowd in a bid to disperse demonstrations and to spread fear. They would pick people off the streets or bundle them out of their homes: the leaders of protests, possible troublemakers, stray protesters, stray children, and the agents of the state would disappear, torture and kill those who fell into their hands. Those who were killed at protests would have their funerals held with great public spectacle. Mourners would arrive in their thousands and would call out revolutionary phrases.

God, Syria, freedom. The people demand the end of corruption. We are no longer afraid.

As the protests deepened, they began to threaten the grip of the state and the grip of the Ba'ath party. In more than one city, at more than one time in mid-2011, Ba'ath party offices were set on fire. Chaos overtook the government. The figurehead prime minister and his cabinet were dismissed and replaced. It made no difference. The state attempted to release a few political prisoners as a gesture, although it was never precisely clear to whom the gesture was meant to appeal. Meanwhile, the regime, including Assad himself in a televised speech, blamed foreigners and Jews for the demonstrations.

And regime snipers lined up on rooftops across Syria, firing down into crowds. Some of the shootings happened in Latakia, the heartland of the Alawites and a bastion of regime support. This violence was then blamed on 'armed gangs' unleashed by a weakening of the government's hand. Its ambition was, if there had to be chaos, to make it total: to pit every ethnic and tribal group against each other, every religious tradition, every city against its neighbours. If chaos reigned, the regime hoped, more people would seek protection from the state. Whoever held the ring could remain in power—even if the country burnt to the ground.

In late April, Daraa, the city in Syria's south where the revolution was first kindled, was surrounded by the forces of the regime. For a week and a half, Daraa was besieged by 6,000 soldiers with tanks and helicopters. Parts of Daraa were cut off without electricity, water and food, in a foretaste of what the war was soon to bring. Snipers took up positions on the roofs of mosques and took shots at anyone who left their homes. Daraa's Omari Mosque was stormed on April 30; tank shells were fired into the building. Through the rest of the city, the soldiers swept, killing some, and arresting thousands, in a broad campaign of terror and intimidation. Throughout April and into May, even small demonstrations in cities like Homs, the country's third-largest, were set upon. Armed men would jump out of cars or fire down from hiding places on rooftops. The death toll steadily mounted.

One of the early dead of the revolution was a young boy called Hamza Ali al-Khateeb. Al-Khateeb was thirteen years old. He disappeared, and was presumed arrested, on April 29, 2011, at a protest against the attack on Daraa. Al-Khateeb fell into the hands of the Air Force Intelligence. His family looked around as the demonstration dispersed, and he was gone. They never saw him alive again. After two weeks of searching for him, al-Khateeb's family received his body. He had been monstrously tortured. He was covered in burns and cuts and bruises. The secret police had mutilated his genitals. Video and pictures of al-Khateeb's body, taken by his distraught family—within days, they were seen by millions. The revolution had one of its first martyrs.

The regime was prepared to release some people from its dungeons, but they were not peaceful protesters. Instead, these were Islamists and jihadists, released under Decree no. 61 in May 2011, which let out members of the Muslim Brotherhood and other organisations like it from regime prisons. Many of these men, some of whom called themselves 'graduates' of the torture-prisons, went on to become leading figures in groups like the Islamic State (ISIS). Some went on to become ISIS executioners. Why did the regime do this? It was locking enough people up; its prisons were big enough to hold such men. It released them not out of the goodness of its heart but in cynical calculation. If jihadists could take root again, the opposition—from before the revolution and those who had begun to demonstrate since—could be tarred with the brush of extreme religion. It would be all the easier, all the more popular internationally, to put down a movement which contained such men.

In May and June, protests only grew. Each Friday, after prayers, demonstrators would come out in cities and towns across the country. They were undaunted by the violence everyone on the streets knew they now faced. By mid-June, the mask had slipped. The Syrian army besieged Jisr al-Shagur, near the border with Turkey. It openly shot civilians on sight. Those who could leave the country fled across the border, leaving Jisr al-Shagur a depopulated wreck where some defectors from the army fought their former comrades amid the ruins. By the end of June, sieges were ongoing in far-flung cities like Daraa, Deir Ezzor, Maraat al-Numaan—the violence spread all across the country. In increasing panic and disarray, the regime sent its soldiers everywhere, breaking up demonstrations, arresting everyone possible, and trying as hard as possible to stamp out the flames that were catching.

5

IN A TIME OF WAR

For months, fighting men had defected from the regime to join the protests, disgusted by the orders that told them to fire on demonstrators, unwilling to lay siege to their own country, unprepared to fight a civil war against peaceful enemies. On July 29, 2011, as the violence against demonstrations continued, and as the protests only grew, Colonel Riad al-Asaad of the Syrian air force and six other officers announced the formation of a Free Syrian Army, a rebel group largely made up of soldiers who refused to fire on protesters and refused to break up demonstrations with tanks. Al-Asaad said that his new army was intended to protect the people, not to terrorise them, and to achieve freedom and dignity for Syrians. Those members of the Syrian armed forces who remained, who fought the people, al-Asaad said, would be legitimate targets, enemies of the people.

Soon, almost without fanfare, a one-sided war of government forces against civilians turned into a real war. Force was met with force for the first time. Syria's future, of civil war, was now certain. The only thing that could stop it was the failure and fall of the Assad regime.

As the opposition slowly formalised, with rebel governments joining together, and various movements of former regime soldiers and officers banding together, the first of a long series of missed opportunities began. At this time, the momentum was with the demonstrators. The regime had proven it was unwilling to compromise to remain in power; it could only fight to retain office. It would gladly, it signalled very clearly, drown the country in blood; it was Assad or the country would be burnt. The regime was not above taking hostages, including the American journalist Austin Tice, who disappeared into regime custody in 2012 and has not, as of February 2025, been found.

In 2011, odd statements started to emerge from the capitals of the world. Some world leaders called for ceasefires, for humanitarian pauses in the fighting, for all manner of things that world leaders had no ability to impose. Many said that Assad was 'a dead man walking'; others maintained, for years, that 'Assad must go'. But making these predictions was worthless without ensuring that they happened. And no one who said they wanted Syria's war to end wanted it badly enough to do anything at all about it.

Throughout the war, as the fighting grew more and more intense and the crimes committed against Syria's civilians grew more flagrant and barbarous, international agencies and bodies like the United Nations kept up a steady drumbeat of press conferences expressing 'concern' at events. UN representatives wore out the sofas at the Damascus Four Seasons hotel; they gave themselves sores sitting on the ornamental chairs in the Presidential Palace. They wore their voices out giving press conferences in which they said there was 'no military solution'. This was always a delusion, a lie. Because while the diplomats pretended there was no military solution, the people actually fighting the war were sure there was. The solution of the Assad regime was the destruction of its enemies. It would accept nothing less. And of the civil war, one side eventually won, proving their case: there was a military solution after all. There is always a military solution—if you're prepared to make one. This is something the UN functionaries never understood.

On 16 April 2013, forces of the regime carried out a massacre at Tadamon, close to the Othman Mosque near Damascus. Agents of the regime's military intelligence gathered up alleged fighters and alleged civilian collaborators, possibly as many as two hundred of them, and shot them all in cold blood. A regime which could do that could do worse.

On August 21, 2013, the Assad regime attacked a rebel position in Ghouta, near Damascus, with the chemical weapon sarin fired in rockets. First manufactured by the chemists of the Third Reich, sarin is a terrible weapon. Its effects were immediate and horrific. Photographs of the dead, footage of them lined up in rows, footage of the dying, all of this is difficult to see and to describe. There is no definitive number of the dead, but it is at least three hundred, possibly up to 1,700. No government that was not barbaric in its very essence could do this. Chemical weapons work no better than bombs or bullets in killing fighting men. They are far better at killing women and children who hide in cellars or under tables, as the chemical agents tend to be heavier than the air and to collect on ground floors and in basements. The regime's use of chemical weapons put it completely and forever beyond the pale. No government that could do this would ever give up power peacefully. No government that could do this would ever stop until it or the country it wished to rule was destroyed.

The governments which had previously lied that Assad must go, had also said something else. They had said that if the regime used chemical weapons, which it was known to have, this would be a 'red line', after which other action might be appropriate. For a week or two in the summer of 2013, world leaders conned Syria's people that something might be done to arrest the tide of slaughter. Meetings were convened in the Pentagon in Virginia. Civil servants in the Ministry of Defence went home a little later. But this was all a lie. Barack Obama, the American president, had no intention of doing anything to punish this chemical massacre. He subscribed, as he later told the editor of *The Atlantic* Jeffrey Goldberg, to a theory of the Middle East where 'a few smart autocrats' ought to run everything. Some people, in reading that remark, put the emphasis on 'smart'.

But this was wrong. Obama most admired, most wanted autocrats to be in power. They didn't have to be smart. He had already, after his government's inept and insincere arming of some rebel elements within Syria, dismissed all opponents to the regime as 'former farmers or teachers or pharmacists'. Many options theoretically existed to support the Syrian opposition, from providing anti-air weapons to blunt the regime's air force, to striking the regime's chemical weapons programme and its air bases directly. Obama chose to do none of those. He was helped in his decision by the British House of Commons, which voted on August 29, thanks to a series of rapid and unannounced changes of mind by the Leader of the Opposition Ed Miliband, against a motion which held the possibility of taking any 'military action' against the Assad regime.

The Americans later forced a paper-thin deal, with Russian mediation, which claimed that the Assad regime was prepared to give up and decommission its chemical weapons programme. Many diplomats who carried on with this complete charade emerged from it with honours and not a stain on their CVs. The Assad regime continued to use chemical weapons, many times, including at least two (and possibly up to seven) more suspected uses of sarin. It used sarin in Khan Sheikhun in Idlib on 4 April 2017, and a chemical weapon (some consider it likely to be sarin, but there is no consensus) in Douma, on 7 April 2018. Both of these attacks caused mass casualties and prompted belated and only partially effective international strikes on the Assad regime's chemical weapons programme.

All this was documented by the 'Nowhere to Hide' project of the Global Public Policy Institute. It carried on just fine after the deal was supposedly struck after August 2013. The chemical weapons programme only ended with the collapse of the Assad regime in December 2024. In 2013, eleven years before, the most obvious opportunity for foreign powers to act, to change the course of a war which went on to take another million lives, was simply thrown away.

Worldwide, the regime engaged in a massive propaganda campaign that never let up. Its enemies, every one of them, were jihadists in the mould of al-Qaeda. No one else could rule Syria but Assad, and it was foolish for anyone to try. Western journalists found, if they were judged to be suitably kind to the government, that it was easier to get access to the government-controlled parts of Syria than the rebel-held areas. Journalists were invited to visit the presidential palace where they were told that the regime was the only game in town. With their secret police escorts, they were shown around Damascus bars and told that alcohol would be banned if Assad fell from power. Far too many reporters took these government-sponsored trips. Unable to speak to the opposition, many didn't even try. Reporters like Robert Fisk swallowed the regime line on every alleged war crime, on every alleged massacre. When the regime was alleged to have used chemical weapons, tame reporters were despatched to the site of the attack. Cleared of civilians, they wandered about while the chemically unstable molecular traces of what had happened dissolved and broke up around them. Fisk once wondered aloud, in 2017, whether all the symptoms of poisoning with chlorine gas might have been caused by a 'dust storm' making everyone's eyes water.

The propaganda machine lasted for the whole duration of the war and was still going strong just as rebels arrived in Damascus, Assad fled the presidential palace to claim asylum in Russia, and the fifty-year-old regime built by his father finally collapsed about his ears faster than a controlled demolition.

6

THE CRUELTY, THE PITY

The war in Syria was not primarily about the Islamic State (ISIS). But ISIS defined much of the character of the war. Its rapid rise, its brutality, its eventual messy and unfinished defeat—all these were emblematic of the conflict. The Palestinian refugee camp of Yarmouk was in Damascus. After support for the opposition grew among Yarmouk's inhabitants, government-supported militias stormed the camp. They fought the Free Syrian Army, which had grown in strength there, inside Yarmouk in 2012, subjecting the camp to a horrific siege. By 2015, the situation was made worse when ISIS fighters arrived in Yarmouk and took over much of it. In the camp, ISIS executed refugees and ruled by terror. The camp ended up under effective blockade in 2015, with thousands caught in a net between armed groups. Slowly, the population was whittled away by violence. In 2017, Yarmouk was officially evacuated. It remained a depopulated shell inside Damascus, formerly the most populous Palestinian camp in all of Syria.

The war in Syria was a great mess. Foreign fighters, and foreign powers, defined much of its shape and character. From the very beginning of the war, Iran had supported the survival of Assad, who was a key ally and agent of the Iranian regime. Masterminded by Qassem Soleimani, commander of the Islamic Revolutionary Guards Corps—Quds Force, Iran launched a Shia jihad, recruiting foreign fighters from across the world—from Iraq and Lebanon, but also from as far afield as Pakistan and Afghanistan—to fight for Assad. Some of these soldiers were considered elite: Hezbollah, from Lebanon, provided much of the muscle for the Assad regime, and launched many cruel military operations of its own, including the siege of Madaya between 2015 and 2017, in which Hezbollah cut off a rebelling town and subjected it to man-made famine of monstrous character. Other Shia militants, like the Liwa Fatemiyoun from Afghanistan, were used more or less as cannon fodder: badly trained, hardly equipped, poorly paid, their lives thrown away at the behest of others for objectives of which they were ignorant.

Other militias predominated on the regime side. Some were organised under the umbrella of the National Defence Forces, stood up in 2012 as paramilitaries. The NDF were thugs, often criminal elements and street gangs not in uniform. Stories of NDF crimes proliferated and spread widely—rape and murder as incidental actions, almost punctuation, to what observers, Syrian and international, knew to be an orgy of stealing and usurpation. Many described a war in which a different militia had set up a roadblock every few miles along a road, each of them demanding a bribe to let travellers and workers pass. This only grew worse as the war went on and Syria, even the areas of the country theoretically in government hands, became increasingly lawless and without any authority except that of the gun and of force.

More feared than the NDF were the ubiquitous thugs from the intelligence agencies, who took people from their beds and off the streets throughout the war. Those who were taken might turn up later, beaten, bruised, even crippled, but worse happened to those who never returned. They simply disappeared into the local branches of state bodies like Syria's Air Force Intelligence, or vanished into the black holes of prisons like Sednaya, known as a torture factory, as a place of dreadful, unspeakable things and from which few escaped or were released before their eventual liberation. As Syrians were displaced and forced to leave the country, the long tail of those who did not know what had happened to their families grew. In every country where Syrians lived, campaigns sprung up. They demanded to know what had happened to family members who had vanished into Sednaya and other factories of death. Sometimes stories filtered out, but many were left in agony, waiting and hoping, some over a decade, that they might see their husband or father, their brother or sister, their son, or their grandson again.

Islamist groups had fought in Syria's war the moment the space first opened for them: many of them pouring across the border with Iraq—the opposite way they had travelled in the past. One of those groups used to call itself the Islamic State of Iraq. Now, it called itself the Islamic State of Iraq and Syria (ISIS). Another, Jabhat al-Nusra (the Support Front), was affiliated for a time with al-Qaeda. ISIS routed some of Syria's moderate rebels in late 2013 and took over much of the desert in Syria's east. By the beginning of January 2014, ISIS was ready for its great expansion, this time out and into Iraq. It surged over the border from January to June 2014, coming within spitting distance of the Iraqi capital Baghdad, and the capital of the Kurdistan Regional Government in Erbil. Only then, and with the massive use of air strikes by the United States, and after the throwing together of a vast Global Coalition of countries, was the ISIS advance turned around. It took many years to push the terror group back. From September 2014, at Kobani, on the Syrian-Turkish border, a six-month campaign, including a terrible siege, was fought between ISIS and every nearby force—the Kurdish People's Protection Units (YPG), Kurdish assistance from across the Iraqi border, Syrian rebels under the Free Syrian Army umbrella, the worldwide Global Coalition. In a gruelling fight, an axis of ISIS's advance was stopped.

Many in Syria, in ISIS's claimed capital of Raqqa, languished for years under the black banners. Under ISIS rule, people suffered beneath the iron fist of a new kind of law. A law of pure force, where everything was a sin and every sin was punishable by death. In the Islamic State's Syrian capital of

Raqqa, groups like Raqqa Is Being Slaughtered Silently collected and smuggled out information on ISIS rule—the caprice, the corruption, the criminality, looting and terror. At this time, the Islamic State began publicly and viciously executing Westerners who had fallen into its hands. It did this as a recruitment tool and a spur, prompting hundreds of people who lived in the Western world, including some women and some children, to travel to ISIS territory. And the other way, ISIS sent terrorists and inspired others in a bid—through dozens of attacks in the latter half of the 2010s—to set Europe and America ablaze. This was a problem without a solution. ISIS had to be defeated where it was based, in Syria and Iraq, where it gained its physical and propaganda strength, and where its cash came from. But that was not everything.

Europe had and still has a problem of Islamist terrorism—something which occupies much of the time of already overstretched domestic intelligence agencies, and which attaches to formerly safe and ordinary parts of life (Christmas markets, commuting by public transport) memories of past dangers. For some time in 2014 and 2015, more people in Western capitals spoke of ISIS as a threat in propaganda terms—its execution and battle videos were well-edited—than as a military threat. Would the impressionable young fall for ISIS and its impressive media operation? What can we do to convince children that terrorism is not cool? These were serious discussions had in Western capitals. Was it reasonable to call ISIS a perversion of Islam? Precisely which Muslim clerics would sign a fatwa (a religious edict) calling ISIS false Muslims? Focus on these side issues clouded the judgements of Western policymakers and occupied their time with PR trivia.

When the campaign against ISIS began it was a mess of contradictions. Unwilling to commit any soldiers on the ground beyond special forces used to call in air attacks and to conduct the occasional raid on jihadist targets, Operation Inherent Resolve (as it was laughably called) relied upon a series of so-called 'partner forces' to do the actual on-the-ground fighting. Most possible partner forces did not like the terms of the deal—the United States refused to permit Syrian rebel forces to fight the Assad regime—and so did not take it. It was Assad who had burnt their country to the ground, killed their families, made them refugees in their own land, depopulated their homes and stolen what was not nailed down. ISIS lived in the desert and fought largely in Iraq. The two threats were not the same. The Global Coalition solved this disjunction with a great lack of skill: it made, out of almost thin air, its own partner—a new Kurdish-led group to be called the Syrian Democratic Forces (SDF). The SDF was the creation of the Democratic Union Party (PYD), which was founded by leadership elements of the Kurdistan Workers' Party (PKK), which has been considered a terrorist organisation by much of the Western world for many years because of its long-standing insurgency against the Turkish government.

For all the SDF's bravery in fighting and the skill with which it was led, it was never popular in large areas of Syria. And yet it ended the war against ISIS occupying large swathes of Syria, even as the Kurdish leadership angled to do deals with the Assad regime, which many inhabitants of former ISIS-occupied areas had fought a civil war and—before that—staged a revolution to escape. The United States had fought a war against ISIS, and in so doing, it had not destroyed ISIS—which still exists—but it had spared, for a time, Bashar al-Assad.

All the while, the regime was perpetrating atrocities. As ISIS was being pounded by American air power, in 2015 and 2016, the city of Aleppo was falling to the Assad regime and Iran and Russia in one of the bloodiest sieges of the war. The old city was flattened, and millions of people were displaced. Every hospital was destroyed by bombs. Whole neighbourhoods simply ceased to exist in a cascade of smashed masonry. The dead went unburied, encased instead in the ruins of buildings and streets. After more than four years, Aleppo fell in late 2016. It was a massacre.

Soon enough, Turkey intervened in Syria. It had been fighting Kurdish terrorist groups, including the Kurdistan Workers' Party (PKK), some of whose former members led the SDF. Because Assad was still in power, and his rebel enemies were weak because other groups had received the American aid that was on offer, it was easy for Turkey to take over some of these groups. After 2017, Turkey created a new force, the Syrian National Army (SNA), made up of former FSA rebels, who largely did Turkey's bidding and fought against the SDF. By this time the war had thoroughly fragmented, with rebel groups denied American and NATO support; they each competed for lesser patrons like Turkey and Qatar. The more religious groups squabbled, often violently, over whose religion was strongest and more orthodox. Many people were assassinated, and many critics violently silenced. Some of the rebel groups became nothing more than gangsters, a copy—in different clothes and with different regional accents—of the thuggish militias which ran government-controlled Syria.

In Syria's north-west, different Islamist groups jockeyed for power. Jabhat al-Nusra had rebranded more than once to become Hayat Tahrir al-Sham and had seen off many rivals to become increasingly entrenched in Idlib province. As cities across Syria fell and former rebels faced a choice—either they could be deported in green buses far away from home or they could be 'reconciled', with no guarantees of what that meant—the population of Idlib swelled vastly beyond its pre-war heights.

The US picked the SDF as a partner to avoid having to challenge Assad, with which (as with Iran and Russia) the SDF had good relations. America's plan was to run a war against ISIS without getting involved in the things that had caused ISIS—including Assad's policy of empowering ISIS to tar his other rivals with the brush of the Islamic State. Assad assumed that this would lead to the West supporting his regime. The campaign against ISIS liberated one-third of Syria but replaced them with the SDF. It was deeply political, altering the balance of power in the war, and entrenching the SDF (which Turkey believes is tantamount to the PKK) on the Turkish border. Fighting between Turkey and the SDF has been sporadic ever since, but it has been consistent.

This was a great mess, made in Washington; it was not solved even a decade later when the Assad regime fell. If there is to be fighting in Syria in the future, it is likely to be between the Kurdish-led SDF and everyone else over the control of the oil industry of Syria's north and east.

At the end of September 2015, Russia had begun major intervention in the Syrian civil war. Assad was a client of the Russian state, but what followed was greater than the support he had received up to then. Russian aircraft struck rebel positions across Syria, operating out of Hmeimim airbase. All this was justified by the threat of the Islamic State, but the Russian forces wanted to prop up the regime at all costs and against all challengers. Intelligence estimates from the United States and Britain did not vary: they estimate that in 2015 and 2016, when ISIS was growing in strength and much of the world was drawn into fighting the Islamic State, over 90 per cent of Russian air strikes were directed at the non-ISIS rebels that posed the greatest threat to the Assad regime.

The Syrian war was not unique in hospitals being prime targets. But the bombing of hospitals, conducted by the Assad regime's air force and the Russian air force, for many years, was an ever-present feature of the fighting. While the siege of Aleppo raged in 2016, its hospitals were repeatedly destroyed by bombardment. United Nations agencies, including the World Health Organisation, provided the coordinates of medical facilities to the regime and to the Russians throughout the war—supposedly to prevent unintentional strikes. When those sites were hit anyway, and repeatedly, Syrians grew suspicious. The regime and the Russians were bombing them using the information they were given to prevent unintentional attacks. What had been safe zones turned into targets. Those in rebel areas stopped giving the UN the coordinates of their hospitals.

But old habits die hard. Even when the final offensive began in 2024 and the Assad regime began to crumble, the token resistance made by the Russians and the regime included the bombing of hospitals in Idlib, as if their locations were programmed into their guidance systems, regardless of the context or the mission.

Into the gap left by the collapse of medical and rescue infrastructure stepped Syrian Civil Defence, also known as the White Helmets. They were rescuers. These men were never armed. They ran towards the sites of bombings and artillery strikes and pulled those they could from the rubble. The White Helmets also filmed much of what they did, proving the toll paid by civilians for the war's bloody course. Their footage, of men working for hours to pull tiny crying children from the rubble, of the calls growing fainter and fainter, choked by dust, under the collapsed ruins of an apartment building, was difficult to watch. The White Helmets were supported in part by funding from foreign governments and charities, and this put a target on their back. They were lied about—smeared as terrorists without foundation.

Frequently, White Helmets were hit by 'double-tap' strikes, where in the aftermath of a bombing, the attackers waited for rescuers to arrive, and then struck the target again, killing as many of the rescue workers as possible. Hundreds of White Helmets were murdered in this way over the course of the war. But finally, when the regime fell in 2024, the White Helmets were able to move for the first time across the country—to Damascus, in Latakia, where they were greeted as heroes. Their eventual arrival in all parts of the country after the fall of Assad was met with celebration, to an accompaniment of car horns and flashing lights. The regime had said these men were terrorists. This was a lie, and an easily disproven one. In December 2024, the White Helmets took up their new posts as emergency services across Syria.

The White Helmets and other organisations were targeted also because they helped outside bodies investigate war crimes in Syria. The regime could not help but produce reams of paperwork even when it wanted to hide its own activities. Campaigns and international legal observatories did their best to gather information, just in case the regime might fall. I was told when reporting on these campaigns that the prosecution of Assad-era officials, if they were ever caught, would involve more paper than the Nuremberg trials which followed the Second World War, and the trials of the genocidaires of the former Yugoslavia before the International Criminal Court. The White Helmets collected their own evidence, and were first-hand witnesses to regime crimes. This is another reason why the state did not want to leave many of them alive.

With the final rebel-held areas and the fighters there bottled up in Idlib, it seemed as though Syria might be forgotten. For a time, in late 2019 and early 2020, it appeared possible that the massive regime and Russian and Iranian offensive might massacre many of those left in Idlib. But Turkish intervention against regime advances, and a behind-the-scenes deal struck between Turkey's president Erdogan and Russia's Vladimir Putin averted that. The country reverted to a frozen conflict, albeit one in which acts of terror were rife, and hundreds were killed in the average week through bombing from the air and artillery strikes. There was a growing sense among Syrians that they were being forgotten, that despite pushing back ISIS, largely without help or thanks, they were being abandoned and left to their fate— that evil was being permitted to triumph in their country, and Assad was only a few years away from being welcomed back into the diplomatic fold. But the regime was rotten. It had always been rotten. Corruption had eaten away at its heart and rendered it hollow.

PART TWO

THE FALL

'Heaven! Heaven! Our country is heaven!'
Syrian revolutionary song, sung by Abdelbasset al-Sarout

7

RESISTANCE

Throughout Syria's war, the best people died. They died in large numbers. They were often killed first, seemingly pointlessly, by those more violent, worse, than they were. The democrats, the reformers, the civil society activists. They were natural targets. They were too popular, too appealing. They threatened others who wanted to hold power, even if they were only threats by their example. Throughout the war, the violence was casual, and inescapable. Assassinations happened frequently. Some of Syria's greatest activists were too popular for their own good. Violence followed at their heels. One of those men, a hero of Syria, was Raed Fares. He was an artist, and the owner of a pro-democracy radio station, Radio Fresh, which went out to Idlib, Aleppo and Hama provinces. In November 2018, Fares, one of Syria's most visible and visionary pro-democracy activists, was savagely murdered in Idlib, in Syria's north.

It wasn't just Fares who was murdered. Alongside him, his colleague Hammud Junayd, who worked with Fares on his radio station, was also killed. This fitted a pattern. It was part of an ongoing campaign of assassination targeting Idlib's moderates and advocates of democracy.

When Fares was killed, his death elicited shock and sadness across the world. But it surprised very few. He had been threatened before, often: threatened by the Assad regime, threatened by the Islamists and jihadists. Many wanted to kill Fares for what he thought and said. An attempt—unsuccessful but threatening—was made on Fares's life in 2014, and another not long after. He lived in a state of inescapable danger, operating his radio station and doing his activism openly in war, well aware that those who wanted him dead were numerous, various and violent. Fares knew the risks he ran. He knew what his fate would be.

We don't know, even now, who killed Fares. The killers were most likely jihadists. When the deaths of Fares and Junayd were first announced, blame quickly fell on Hayat Tahrir al-Sham. HTS was then a jihadist group previously affiliated with al-Qaeda (HTS had formally severed ties with al-Qaeda in 2016), and its thugs were broadly deemed responsible. But, Fares's friends said openly, the killers could, on any other day, have received their orders from the Islamic State, or another jihadist group operating in Syria. They could have been agents of the regime of Bashar al-Assad; members of the regime's National Defence Force (NDF) militias; the Russian soldiers and mercenaries; or Iranian assets. It could have been any of them. So widely were Fares, Junayd and other moderates like them hated by Syria's violent men.

Fares's death was so tragic not only because it was the end of his extraordinary life, but because it said something about Syria's war. The conflict had degenerated by that point. Fares's life and the story of his doomed efforts spoke volumes. With Fares gone, it was more apparent than ever that the dark forces he opposed seemed to be gaining in strength and by 2017, his killers appeared to be winning in Syria.

To understand the tragedy of these murders, one needed only to look at Fares's and his colleagues' work. They wanted a liberated country, a democracy. Radio Fresh and Fares's other efforts were committed to a free Syria. He and Junayd followed this cause even if the pursuit of that idea took their lives. They were figures of hope not only in their home country but for democrats and reformers across the world. Fares's mission could and did easily attract the most grandiose labels. It was necessarily heroic. Its morality was world-bestriding.

There was a small irony. Fares was famous, but he was not a celebrity activist. Many Syrians were abroad, and there was a world-wide audience for his work, but Fares did not occupy the global circuit as other celebrity activists have done. His politics were local as much as they were global, centred around his home village of Kafr Nabel and his home province of Idlib.

On his radio station, Radio Fresh, which was supported, until that support was cut off a few months earlier, by some American money, Fares sent out his message. The radio station provided news on Syria's war and satirised its worst participants—jihadists and regime alike. Radio Fresh faced intimidation and contended constantly with the prospect of closure. The jihadists, for their part, could not stand Fares's radio station playing music, which they had banned.

Fares had more than a radio station. His work included innovative banners and signs, often written in English, often referencing popular culture and recent events, which attempted to draw Syria closer to the watching world. They were world famous, the banners from Kafr Nabel. Fares wrote the banners himself, invoking Syrian empathy with other people's suffering. The most poignant examples included Kafr Nabel's response to the 2013 Boston Marathon bombing, in which a city ravaged by war shared its condolences with Americans struck by terrorism, and its heartfelt condemnation of the murder of the journalist James Foley at the hands of ISIS. 'Humanity is proud of James', the banner read.

For many years, the only good that was done in Syria's war was done on a local level. With his radio station and with his media activism, Fares was part of that movement of civil society. He put into practice a theory of local democracy which was the closest rebel Syria came at that time to freedom. This localism was adopted only later. The rebels had brighter visions for many years. But after the world whose goodwill Fares sought let Assad get away with murder, things changed. The world underwrote the survival of

Assad's regime. The 'international community' (a complete fiction) decided that freedom for the whole of Syria could not come about in the face of worldwide indifference. Fares never accepted that as a fact.

This is what Fares argued. The world had abandoned Syria. But that did not mean all was hopeless. Those who retained some freedom to act, in whatever small ways they had left, had a duty to do so. His idea was liberating Syria village by village, town by town, extricating whatever they could, no matter how small, from the dual tyrannies of Ba'athism and jihadism. Fares said that they had to do this for the sake of their children.

That is how many would like to remember Fares. A photograph taken not long before his murder had Fares standing in Kafr Nabel in late September with his sons. The green, white and black stripes with red stars, the colours adopted by Syria's revolution, were around his shoulders. Fares was demonstrating against the dark forces who brought his violent death not long after. It was clear then that Fares's murder made something obvious, painfully so. Tyranny and terror will always attempt to crush all opposition. Unchecked by some serious force, of course, they will succeed.

It was years in the making, the killing of someone like Fares and the bid to destroy his organisation. In a war, in any situation of extended internecine violence and civil conflict, the extremes are allowed to grow in strength. This meant their enemies, the moderates, were at great risk. Moderates not only found themselves under pressure from both sides. They were inevitable targets because they held a natural legitimacy and exhibited nobility which extremists and regime sympathisers both envied and sought to destroy.

It was virtually inevitable that Fares would, in the course of his work, meet a violent end. He knew it but kept going regardless, his optimism and hope finally running out. His life said something about what was allowed to happen to Syria by a world whose morality Fares tried so hard and, in his lifetime, failed to spur.

8

POISON

Chemical weapons defined Syria's civil war. Before sarin, a Nazi-era nerve agent, was used in August 2013 in Ghouta, near Damascus, the Western world had declared that the use of chemical weapons by the Assad regime would cross a 'red line'. What stepping over the line might mean was left unsaid. Syrian activists and their friends believed something significant: they believed that Assad would be overthrown if he used those weapons. The nations of the world claimed they were very worried about chemical weapons. The last dictator who used them widely was Saddam Hussein, and he was overthrown by the Americans and executed by the new Iraqi government for his crimes.

The same did not happen to Bashar al-Assad. In August 2013, the air in Ghouta, near Damascus in Syria, was made fatal to breathe by a chemical agent. Over a thousand—we still do not know the exact number—choked horribly to death in awful pain. As with all chemical weapons, the sarin used by the regime of Bashar al-Assad on this rebellious suburb was more effective on civilian targets, seeping into the places where people who were not fighting had hidden. It was better at killing innocents than it was at suffocating a front line of fighting men.

The children the weapon reached were too small to escape the heavy air, which clung to the ground. Many women, some of them doomed by traditions of modesty, were not hosed down fast enough to remove the chemical agent from their bodies. Video taken of these events is unbearable to watch. It is unbearable to read about. The footage, shot a little later, of so many of them lying there dead, row after row of bodies, is even when you have seen it many times, many times over many years, impossible to believe. All of those lives ended for nothing. It was so senselessly cruel.

Almost as cruel as the mass murder was the propaganda which surrounded it. One lie travelled around the world before many of the victims had died. Instantaneously, as the chemical weapon was first reported on the news wires, the Assad regime and its allies in Russia, Iran and China began to claim that the attack that everyone had seen and observed on video did not happen. They later said that the test results of chemical samples smuggled out of the country did not mean anything either. Our eyes, ears and laboratory equipment were all lying. Nothing of the kind had happened in Ghouta that day.

This is what the regime and its allies claimed. First, they said, it wasn't a chemical attack. Or, it was a chemical attack but the chemical used was not sarin. Or, it was a chemical attack, but it was carried out by America, Turkey, or the rebels themselves. They said anything that occurred to them, regardless of whether it was plausible or not. They introduced so many theories that propagandists for the regime, and credulous old journalists like Seymour Hersh, didn't know which line to parrot.

If these theories all sound mutually contradictory, they were. If these excuses seem desperate and grasping, that's because they were. This was a bid to lie not by accuracy or plausibility but by volume. The lies spread so far and so widely that they still survive to this day, twelve years later. It is an article of faith in many parts of the world thousands of miles from Syria that this chemical attack, which is beyond any factual dispute, did not happen. In Brian Whitaker's book about this subject, *Denying the Obvious*, the author surveys the landscape of alternative theories and decides that they are all post-hoc, feeble, and built more on the mutual reinforcement of unreconcilable trivia, and the psychological need to believe, than a reckoning with the facts. Facts are boring, even when over a thousand die. A conspiracy is significantly more fun. And that is why it is believed. The lies never could fit all the facts, but that was hardly the point. All it had to do was cast doubt on any claims that negatively reflected on Assad. That is all these lies were for. The chemical attack was soon no more than a news-themed choose-your-own-adventure. So determined were so many factions and sub-factions to defend the Assad regime from the possibility of retribution, that they used whatever tactic they could. Everything was grist for their mill.

In the years since, two other large-scale chemical attacks caught international attention: in Khan Sheikhun in April 2017, and Douma a year later. Idle for years, but with a growing toolkit, the regime's allies, defenders and agents reacted. They jumped in, offering reasons why these attacks, too, could not possibly have been committed by the only armed force capable of committing them. The only combatant in Syria with an air force that could drop canisters full of chemical agents. No one polls this question, but millions of Americans likely believe, even now, that there either were no chemical attacks in Syria, or, if there were, that anyone but Assad's men committed them.

As before: a catalogue of evasions, lies, or excuses for why—if the regime had used chemical weapons—it would have been ultimately justified. Since August 2013, all of these ideas percolated in millions of minds. Some facts, now: The Syrian civil war has been fought for thirteen years. In that time, the regime was alleged to have used chemical agents, not once or twice, but many hundreds of times. A series of reports, called the Nowhere to Hide project, from the Global Public Policy Institute, which remains the benchmark for study of the subject, has in total collated 349 uses of chemical agents by the regime.

To doubt this tide of evidence does not make you informed or savvy. It makes you beholden to the lies of others, and a fool of your own making. In

2013, all of this was hard to predict. Things changed. When Assad first used chemical weapons, it was to survive. During the ten years that followed Syria's war, it was only relatively late that informed opinion—especially among the Arab states and their diplomats—concluded that the regime would not be forced from power. Even after Russia intervened to save the regime in December 2015, the intelligent people (and the intelligence agencies) insisted that this was a last-minute rescue mission, and would conclude with Assad being elbowed aside in favour of a more acceptable regime figure, who could begin to reach a negotiated settlement. What people forgot then was the effect that using weapons of mass destruction successfully—without retribution—has on a regime and a leader.

Saddam Hussein did the same thing. He got away with using chemicals to murder in war and against civilians, and therefore thought that he was special, given celestial permission, and was beyond the reach of consequences and the law. In August 2013, the president of the United States and the British parliament derailed any attempt to punish the Assad regime for its use of chemical weapons, or to use force to prevent the next chemical attack.

The Obama administration fell for an eleventh-hour plan from Russia, of all countries, which claimed it wanted to disarm the regime's chemical arsenal. The Obama administration was completely played, played like the biggest fools on the planet. For years afterwards, and even in their memoirs, these officials maintained that this transparent con job had been a fantastic piece of diplomacy on their part, even as the other chemical attacks mounted up—and the US, France and Britain in 2017 and 2018 struck the regime to damage its surviving chemical infrastructure.

At the time, others predicted that Ghouta would license more sabre-rattling and more violence from America's enemies, who scented weakness and saw a Western Alliance divided and captive to an inferiority complex. Intelligent people demurred and said that things don't work like that. Russia invaded Ukraine in 2014, in the first salvo of what became a full-scale war, an attempt at wholesale annihilation, in 2022. Russia's 2014 invasion happened seven months after the chemical attack on Ghouta. Again, the intelligent people said: we don't know that Russia's invasion of Ukraine and Assad's successful use of chemical weapons are related. We simply cannot attribute one thing to the influence of the other.

But people do take their cues from other things that happen, whether or not our expert class believes they should. Russia detected that we now live in a world of impunity, and invaded Ukraine on that basis. Years later, seven months after the Taliban overthrew the Afghan government, and humiliated the United States and NATO, in August 2021, Russia invaded Ukraine again, this time with annexation on its mind. In the past ten years, it had used chemical weapons to try to assassinate Russian exiles in Britain, in the Skripal poisonings in Salisbury which had left one woman, Dawn Sturgess, dead. The poison of Syria's civil war, untreated, uncontained, spread out and spread very far.

9

PROPAGANDA

The year 2022 was the season for diplomacy in the Middle East, even for the most distasteful of leaders. Joe Biden, then the American president, paid a visit to Saudi Arabia in July, against his own inclinations as he had a long-standing dislike of the Saudi state. Biden did it because of the need to lower oil prices. American and European diplomats scrambled hopelessly to reach a new nuclear deal with Iran, one which was not made.

Barely beneath these movements towards diplomatic rehabilitation, however, was an especially unsavoury element: the possible reintegration, by stealth, of this century's most significant mass murderer, and the coming in from the cold of one of the world's most offensive pariah states. From 2020 on, and more successfully from 2022, Bashar al-Assad slowly weaselled his way back onto the international circuit. After years of a diplomatic boycott, Assad began a campaign of foreign visits and efforts in 2020 to rejoin institutions like the Arab League and others that had suspended Syria's membership while he was in power. They had done so for perfectly good reasons: because of his human rights abuses and war crimes. The prisons and the death camps were in 2022 still open. Yet Assad believed, with some reason, that his fellow leaders no longer cared about any of that.

The trips poured in. Assad was seen in Tehran and the United Arab Emirates, with another visit to Moscow, the Syrian dictatorship's closest ally, per year. In Tehran, Assad met with then-Iranian president Ebrahim Raisi and Iran's Supreme Leader Ali Khamenei, with state media from both Iran and Syria trumpeting incipient improvements in bilateral relations. Once upon a time, the United Arab Emirates had called for Assad to go. Almost overnight, it had become one of his strongest supporters. From 2016 onwards, the UAE sent steadily more diplomats and officials to Damascus, advocated for Assad to be readmitted to international institutions, and lobbied the Arab world to recognise Assad and to give his regime money. Money for reconstruction, it was said. But in the years after, until the regime's fall in 2024, precious little was rebuilt or reconstructed except the fortunes of those connected with the Assad regime.

In the UAE in 2022, Assad met the then-deputy supreme commander of the armed forces, Mohammed bin Zayed (known as MBZ), who is now president. The two discussed euphemistically, political and humanitarian support for Syria—in other words, the provision of both economic and political capital to allow the Assad regime to take its place once more among the recognised Arab nations. The Emirates for years led the campaign to have Syria's suspension from the Arab League lifted; they attempted to start investment forums and to create reconstruction funds from which the regime could draw. The UAE authorities went some way to push pro-Assad propaganda around this visit, and to boost their government's efforts to rehabilitate him. They claimed that Assad and his 'wise leadership,' no less, must be accepted back into the diplomatic fold—partly as a fait accompli; but also because they believed Syria must be rebuilt under Assad's rule. Per official statements going back to 2016, this was part of an Emirati strategy to wean Assad off his Iranian allies, whose proxy forces were not only entrenched within Syria, but who were integral to the survival of the regime. Meanwhile, the Emiratis in their state media said they could separate Iran from Assad, and do deals with both.

In parallel, the UAE also courted Russia amid its invasion of Ukraine, with MBZ glad-handing Putin in Moscow. Even Turkey—now considered a great steadfast friend of Syria's opposition—made some overtures to Assad. Turkish diplomatic sources and analysts insisted then that Turkish president Erdogan would never normalise with Assad. He had demanded that Assad go many times, and called for his defeat. And Turkish forces fought to a standstill a major Assad regime advance in 2020. But with the balance within Syria in chronic flux—especially as Russian forces redeployed following the invasion of Ukraine—there was an increased demand from all parties to Syria's conflict to secure their own interests. Erdogan himself declared his willingness to meet with Assad, and that such a meeting would happen 'when the time is right'.

Turkey wanted in 2022 what it wants now, in 2025: to control the north of Syria. In 2025, Turkey says the things it said in 2022, as it had done in the past: that it is about to launch an offensive into the Kurdish-controlled areas of Syria's northeast. Assad had for many years wished to co-opt the Kurdish areas controlled by the Democratic Union Party (PYD), and to bring them into his shaky alliance system—one the UAE hoped to stabilise with cash and diplomacy. Now Assad is gone, but Turkey's goals remain the same.

In 2022 it was clear that, if those countries wanted peace, wanted stability, this stability could not come through dealing with Assad. Assad was dependent on military help from outsiders. And Syria's economy, never strong before, was shattered—with chronic shortages, high prices and a broken labour market. All this meant Assad used diplomacy to chase foreign funds. While Assad was in the UAE, it was fancifully alleged he would cross the border into Saudi Arabia to discuss the crisis in Lebanon. Another rumour had it that he might make his return to the diplomatic arena with trips to Qatar and former Soviet countries.

But Syria's civil war kept rumbling on, with hundreds killed each month, with continual exchanges of fire on the supposedly frozen front lines. New and old atrocities of the regime's prison system were exposed almost monthly. Hundreds of thousands of political prisoners had disappeared into the regime's prison archipelago—and this was widely known. In May 2022, a rumour spread that many were due to be released. Thousands of families, clutching photographs of their missing relations, petitioned for their return. The amnesty that followed freed, at most, a few hundred. The rest continued to languish in jail. Most of the missing were already dead.

The official UN count of the dead in Syria's civil war concluded at only half a million, but most reasonable observers think the toll is more than double that. The UN Office for the High Commissioner on Human Rights estimated civilian casualties at over 300,000. The vast majority of civilian casualties in the war (90 percent, according to monitors like the Syrian Network for Human Rights) occurred at the hands of the Assad regime and its Russian and Iranian allies.

Even setting morality aside, bringing Assad into the community of nations was always a bad idea. In economic terms, regime-held Syria was a basket case. It rationed everything. The official exchange rate was so distorted compared to the black market one that it was almost comical. This is where the propaganda came in.

Syria was at war for fourteen years. Much of its cities were destroyed. A good deal of the country's ancient and medieval history was flattened by repeated bombardments. But this did not keep all the tourists away. Countries in war can make surprising tourist destinations. Syria was one of them. This was one objective of the Assad regime. It wanted to forge greater ties with the rich world, even as its war against the people of Syria continued. Thus, the regime continued to suggest that it was a great tourist destination. It did its best to maintain an incongruous association with leisure and travel. Until the regime fell in late 2024, a surprisingly large but carefully chosen number of foreigners vacationed in Syria.

It hoped the visitors would paint a picture of a country at liberty and peace, not at war. Bars full, evening spots and nightclubs jumping. If all went to plan, they could overlook the destruction and depopulation of cities like Aleppo and Homs and the prominent posters of Bashar al-Assad and his father Hafez that predominated even among the ruins. For many of those travelling to Syria, this is exactly what they did. They marvelled at its ancient history. They danced in the hottest clubs. Some foreigners were admitted on scarce tourist visas and conducted, for a significant fee, by government-approved fixers around Syria's major cities, as well as historic sites that occupy a small but significant place in state propaganda.

Others, including those in the media and people with political and cultural connections, were toured by bus around the country. They were shown model classrooms and, on occasion, smiling schoolchildren. They met with figures associated with the regime—including the then-grand mufti of Syria, Ahmed Badreddin Hassoun, who had (in addition to his religious duties) been signing death warrants. Hassoun was an old professional. He would take the hands of visitors, including one I have interviewed, stare deep into their eyes, and say that he believed he and they had a profound spiritual connection. Other visitors would meet, at the regime's behest, supposedly independent 'journalists', who lectured them on why Assad was a wonderful president and his survival was essential. Everyone these visitors met gave the regime's official line on civil conflict.

In April 2018, one such tour took shape. It was led, if not directed, by a British baroness, Caroline Cox of the House of Lords, and included minor politicians, journalists, and the British Anglican priest Giles Fraser. I spoke to some on the tour. Its moments of absurdity were documented by a member of the group, the reporter Gareth Browne, who wrote a series of dispatches for *The National*, the United Arab Emirates newspaper, describing what Cox called 'the crazy club' on its travels around regime-controlled Syria. At one moment, the tour group presented their bemused regime minders with cheap souvenirs from Westminster. At another, they were addressed in an official setting by Vanessa Beeley, a conspiracy theory blogger who was assumed to speak for the regime, despite claiming to have no association with it.

Another tour went around Syria not long after. They got less press coverage. That group included American writers and activists, some of whom were then employed by Russian state-aligned media. It was centred on attempts to demonstrate a Syria at peace and leisure under the Assad regime. Social media posts by the group showed views of locations such as Sednaya, which housed a notorious prison where many thousands of people were then alleged (and are now known) to have been killed and dismembered by the state. Other posts showcased the number of bars that had apparently opened in the old city of Damascus.

The regime's opponents, when they were mentioned by people on these trips, were described as jihadists who sought and failed to tamp down the desire of Syrians of opposite sexes to consume alcohol and cohabit before marriage. Other tours by French and British far-right figures struck similar notes. Thierry Mariani, a member of Marine Le Pen's far-right National Rally party, tweeted when he went around Syria on regime-organised tours about the French wine he was enjoying near Sednaya. Nick Griffin, who was formerly leader of the British National Party, made many trips to Syria in a similar vein.

These journeys coalesced around similar themes. One was the Syrian regime's desire to associate itself with Western-style amusements, such as bars and nightlife, in contrast to the death and violence with which its forces were most commonly associated. And sanctions. The tours were all about sanctions. The aim of the tours was also to suggest that all misery, privation and poverty in Syria was the product of international sanctions against the Assad regime. Propagandists of this type said sanctions were an undeclared war against Assad and, because he was the state, all Syrians—with graver economic consequences for Syrians than a decade of war itself had brought. Thus, Assad must be given sanctions relief immediately, the tourists declared. It was only fair. It was only just.

Even without making these points explicitly, those who toured the country uncritically served to cement propaganda themes. Syrian opposition figures and human rights activists criticised those who took Assad regime accommodation, travel expenses, or freebies. But they wondered something else. What effect did these propaganda tours have? Did they help the regime when it needed international approval most of all?

When the Assad regime finally fell, people who toured the country with the regime changed their tunes. Where once they'd travelled around Assad's Syria and said how safe and wonderful it was, now they sounded a little bit more reserved. One or two of them went back to Syria in the chaos of liberation. Some even toured regime sites after the regime fell: presidential palaces, drug laboratories, prisons. A few looked not at all abashed as they went around the places where the man whose coin they had taken had produced narco-pills by the million. Wow, one or two of them said in YouTube videos. Wow.

It's hard to find yourself on the losing side. Will Syrians forgive those who visited their country on the regime's behalf? Every Syrian I have discussed this with is adamant. They want tourism to return to their country. They want everyone possible to visit Syria. Of course, everyone who visited Syria at the regime's behest is welcome to return to a country free of Assad. They are welcome to visit and to spend their money. But the people who provide them food and lodging may not entirely look them in the eye.

10

SYRIA'S WAR, ON DRUGS

Modern war is a racket. In civil wars fought across the world, parties to the conflict are often armed groups, operating according to their own rules. These groups are often concentrated around a small area, or among members of an individual ethnicity or tribe, or those professing a particular creed. The leaders of these groups often behave like brigands and mafiosos, demanding protection money and extorting those in the land under their control, meanwhile scheming to overtake the territory of other, competing warlords.

Even the proxy forces of regional powers, some of them well-funded, resort to looting, and other crimes, to supplement their salaries—as do the soldiers of weak states, like the regime of Bashar al-Assad. The regime resorted to its fair share of kidnapping, blackmail, demands for protection money, and straight theft. When the Assad regime took a town, a Syrian joke went, everything which has not been flattened by Russian bombs was likely to be 'liberated' in subsequent mass looting. Starting with the washing machines. They were always the first to go. The Syrian Arab Army (the army of the Assad regime) was more effective against a room full of white goods than it was against any real opponent. This joke circulated for ten years. It did the rounds again in late 2024, when the regime fell apart in a week and a half. The state had been rotten all along.

But theft is only one crime armed groups engage in to enrich themselves. Another is even more comparable to the modus operandi of a mafia: the trafficking of narcotics. The regime of Bashar al-Assad was one of the most prolific drug traffickers of this century. We see it in case after case, all around the Mediterranean Sea. A record-breaking shipment of amphetamines was seized by Italian authorities on its way from Syria in 2020. Italian police said they seized up to 14 tons of amphetamines, 84 million tablets, estimated to have a rough value of $1 billion. Just in that one shipment alone. Ever since this seizure, the exact ownership of the drugs has been debated, though not that it was someone in the Assad regime. Just as it did for any number of drug cases across the region. They all pointed back to the grubby warehouses in the southern Syrian countryside, that's where the drugs were being made.

Syria's war is powered by the cheap stimulant called captagon. Amphetamines have seen extensive use in war and, like its predecessors, captagon keeps fighters active long beyond the limits of ordinary endurance. They feel invincible, shrugging off eventually fatal wounds. Syria's war was one in which many groups mounted suicide attacks. On the battlefield, the drug makes fighters alert on dreary watches; it gives them false courage and stops the most debilitating effects of pain. Captagon had its place. And there was a recreational side. In the same way that drugs often find new popularity amid the hopelessness of warfare, captagon is also widely used for escape, for fun, in Syria as well as across the Middle East. The advantages are legion.

The shipment intercepted by Italian authorities was one of the largest ever seized. And Italy's police first said it was down to ISIS—something authorities are always keen to suspect and to allege. In theory, this was not impossible. ISIS fighters made use of the drug themselves and have operated lucrative sidelines in the theft of antiquities which requires international smuggling and sale. But to crack the case, more detective work was required. And the claim that this was an ISIS drug shipment now seems unrealistic. Indeed, the attribution of all this to the Islamic State was questioned at the time by Daniele Raineri, an Italian journalist, and Sam Dagher, the author of *Assad or We Burn the Country*, a definitive history of Syria's war. Italian authorities have since minimised the ISIS connection.

Our theoretical detective noticed the following. The three ships from which the tablets were seized came from Latakia, a port controlled then by the regime of Bashar al-Assad. The theoretical detective might have intimated that this necessitated a regime connection to the shipment. It soon seemed far more likely that this shipment was the product of deals made between Hezbollah, the Assad regime, other pro-regime militias, and the Naples mafia. This connection may at first have seemed strange, but it is hardly as unusual as it sounds. When one wishes to sell drugs from a warzone, the expertise of organised crime marries almost perfectly to those of a sectarian militia or a rogue state short of cash. Criminals know other criminals by sight. They are always ready to make a deal of this kind with willing partners.

And Hezbollah was not new to the drugs racket. Hezbollah and other Iranian proxies have had a long history of drug-trafficking as a way to earn revenue. It's something Hezbollah unconvincingly denies. Its leaders say to this day that it goes against their religion. But American Treasury officials and analysts have long said that Hezbollah uses the proceeds of criminal activity across the world—including the sale of drugs—to buy illegal weapons for its fighters and to mount foreign operations. Its involvement in the Syrian captagon trade would not represent anything new, or different, to the men who managed Hezbollah's broader trade in drugs.

Our Italian detective thinks. There was evidence to suggest that Hezbollah was producing drugs in Lebanon until recently, and that this was something the Assad regime encouraged from across the border. Now, the production and sale of captagon and other drugs proved to be crutches for Syria's shattered war-ravaged economy, and selling amphetamines abroad could, the regime thought, increase revenues further.

In 2020, the situation in Syria was bad: many of those fighting were hooked on drugs which made them more prone to violence and less willing to give up when fighting starts. The drug trade undermined the rule of law, empowered militia leaders, and shifted money away from the real economy, the legitimate economy. Even interrupting and impounding shipments seemed futile; the drug trade continued—as surely enriching the mafiosos and aiding the warlords as would a descent into further conflict.

The regime of Bashar al-Assad, even when it was unlikely to be overthrown, had become the Middle East's biggest moocher, the biggest sponge—a drug-dealing entity which begged with one hand for 'reconstruction' funds from nearby monarchies to keep its own corrupt machinery in operation, while stealing from the population of foreign countries by selling them pills that would hook them in the short term, kill them in the long.

Wartime brings its own economic calculations. In Syria, as old authority disintegrated and civil society buckled, what was once illegal and punished became lucrative and practical. In war, the 'dark' or illegal economy soon vacuums up labour and capital. In Syria, this included the widespread manufacture and selling of illegal drugs, including hashish and captagon.

Captagon carries serious risks. It causes lasting physical and neurological damage and it can kill by overdose. Its ramshackle and criminal manufacture means the quality of drugs supplied is uncertain and frequently dangerous. As several recent reports document, the production of this drug has changed during the course of the war. Where once, as Caroline Rose and Alexander Söderholm document in a major study for the New Lines Institute called 'The Captagon Threat', production was concentrated, small-scale, in some areas, later the drug was manufactured in industrial quantities in government territory, with the increasingly overt approval of the regime.

The drug lords were the warlords, and they operated like cartel captains. Maher al-Assad, the younger brother of Bashar, was the chief producer and pusher of the drug. He ran the army's Fourth Division and all its criminal activities. He had a drug factory in al-Basa, Latakia governorate. He had manufacturing hubs along the Syria and Lebanon border region. After the regime fell, Maher al-Assad's factories were toured by awed journalists filming everything with their phones. Cement mixers and chemicals for making the batches. Great big sacks filled with pills, ready for shipment. It was an industrial business.

Wasim Badia al-Assad is a cousin of Bashar al-Assad who controlled local militias in Latakia province. Bald and bearded, Wasim was said to have trafficked the pills from the factories to the state-owned ports, making sure no one stopped the shipments on their way. Other businessmen allegedly involved in the trade included Rami Maklouf, billionaire cousin of Bashar al-Assad whose children fancied themselves Instagram influencers. And Khodr Taher, a local businessman with fingers in a lot of pies. Amer Khiti was a member of the Syrian People's Assembly (the country's fake parliament before its closure once the regime fell) and had businesses in livestock, property, shipping and transport. Like many a mob boss, he worked in construction, too. His packaging facilities were affiliated with massive captagon smuggling operations from Latakia's ports.

With Syria's legitimate primary and secondary industries in states of disarray and collapse, captagon became a serious export. Allying with criminal networks across the region, Assad's Syria exported captagon in creative ways, and at an eye-popping scale. Foreign jurisdictions routinely seized millions of pills—sometimes hidden in crates of fruit, or run directly across borders at high speed. The Jordanian military, which in 2022 alone seized 16 million captagon pills, is increasingly open on the subject of its growing war with the smugglers. It advertises that its soldiers and border guards follow a new policy: shooting to kill on sight.

The vast majority of these drugs were neither spotted nor seized. They simply couldn't be, given the scale and seriousness of the drug economy that emanated from Syria. In trying to explain their confiscations, foreign countries were sometimes at a loss. The problems of black markets and the illicit smuggling of unregulated substances were real enough, as were the clear links to international organised crime. Like Italy, Jordan sometimes says, for lack of knowledge, lack of an alternative, that it was ISIS who did the smuggling, not Assad. But the other manufacturers and beneficiaries were hardly better than the Islamic State. The results of their drug smuggling were no less brutal. Their markets were in the Mediterranean and the Persian Gulf. Jordan's military happened to be in between Syria and these markets.

Syria's emergence as a narco-state had broad implications. The drugs themselves were social and political menaces for Syria's many neighbours. They wrecked and shortened lives. But so did the infrastructure they required and rewarded. The drug trade produced drug smugglers and drug gangs. It made a drug gang out of what was once a government. Growing out of a pre-existing war, these gangs armed themselves and fought. They fought each other, and anyone representing the law. Syria for some years resembled a kind of cartel-riven Mexico or Colombia, with the drug gangs increasingly well-armed, increasingly rich and powerful, increasingly going their own way. The fall of the Assad regime interrupted their sweet little deal. But they may well soon be back. They will be a serious challenge for the new powers that now rule in Damascus.

Over the past few years, there were numerous instances of violence between drug gangs within the Syrian state and its allies, and violence against border posts and law enforcement in Lebanon and Jordan. All this violence resulted conservatively in dozens of deaths. One incident on Christmas Day 2021 catches the eye: Jordan's armed forces fought as many as 200 Syrian smugglers carrying machine guns who were trying to enter Jordan from Suweida and Daraa provinces. It was a new drug war, open as anything. The dead of this new war included Jordanian and Lebanese soldiers, border guards, policemen—and some of the smugglers themselves. Not to mention the civilians caught up in the trade.

Work from the Organized Crime and Corruption Reporting Project indicated widespread drug-related corruption within the Assad regime. We can infer not only that the regime was complicit in this growing drug trade, but also that much of its nominally legitimate economic and political functions were either connected to or subsumed within the criminal world of drug production. With rough estimates indicating that the captagon trade was worth more than $5 billion to Syria in 2021 alone, there was no reason for a criminal regime in search of money to swear off the means of getting more.

Assad claimed his government was a stabilising influence, and as he toured the Middle East region in pursuit of diplomatic normalisation and economic reconstruction, he claimed he was a suitable partner for all manner of initiatives. He said he needed large sums of money to participate fully, of course. But a state built anew on these foundations—of corruption and illegality, and with violence entrenched in its drug economy—could never stabilise itself. The regime was rotten to the core. Its collapse in 2024 only proved what so many already knew.

With organised crime, terrorist organisations, and armed militias all participating in this black market, the regime made a rod for its own back. The regime hollowed out the state, turned bureaucrats and soldiers into criminals and thieves. And then when it was beaten like a defeated gang, sent running like a bunch of criminals, the regime itself seemed almost surprised. But it made its own bed. It collapsed itself. When Assad fell, Syria's drug trade had claimed another victim.

11

THE EARTHQUAKE

On the sixth of February 2023, both Syria and Turkey were struck by a terrible earthquake. For Syria, the earthquake was a horror atop horrors, an insult after a decade of cruel insults. The country had possibly allowed itself to think it had seen its fill of rubble. After a decade of war, cities which had not been rebuilt lay ghostly and empty and choked with dust. Overcrowded refugee camps in the north and east gave little shelter or security to their inhabitants. Warplanes and artillery bombarded those areas at the periphery of the country where millions of dispossessed were forced to live. All of this before the new violence of an act of god.

What was reported about the earthquake almost defied description—even though these things had happened before in the Middle East, in other earthquakes. Entire communities vanished from the map. Settlements, streets, and whole villages disintegrated around and over their residents. Children and whole families are buried beneath their houses. Observers saw time run out to save survivors who were trapped under fallen structures, hiding in air bubbles. Syrian contacts posted photographs of lost friends. Some photographed themselves standing before coffins. The pleas for information about cousins and uncles, nieces and nephews, then stopped as hope was given up. Soon afterwards, requests for information began to be taken down. Not much was known, but much was sadly presumed.

The earthquake was so horrific it was impossible to think about it directly and straight. The world did not listen and instead focused either on the hyper-specific—a miracle baby, born and rescued from under the rubble—or the general: a DEC campaign, a Red Cross campaign, demands and indignant yelps to lift the sanctions and to give the country's tyranny, still then in power, what it wanted.

Friends told me that to see property developers in Turkey—the people who built up and sold on the structures which so catastrophically failed their inhabitants—clapped in irons, which did eventually happen, was a privilege and a thrill. The hope was that these people will be made to take the rap and face the consequences. Even if this is a political shifting of blame from an embattled government, it is something: justice in a word, vengeance in another.

In Syria, the same thing was not possible. In part, this was the political economy of the Assad regime—its corporatism meant that the business and political elite were one and the same, and the whole system existed to wash money through the shell of a country into the pockets of the select; and that this could never result in justice, never punishment, for everyone in power was as buried in corruption as the poor are now buried in the ruins of their homes. This was the story of the Assad regime, one which possibly came to an end when it fell.

It's worth thinking about the sort of country Syria was before the fall of the regime, especially the north, which the occasional journalist was only briefly able to visit. Mile upon mile of ruins. A local population inured to a certain kind of suffering, now forced to confront the bitter realities of another. Syria remained an open sore. Part of the wound is visible still. A problem whose very lack of resolution for so many years had made whatever happened next—good or, as in this case, unspeakably bad—far worse.

Much of the construction in Syria under Assad was monopolised by oligarchs close to the regime. Samer Foz, a business magnate, was accused of profiting from funds earmarked for Syria's reconstruction when he was sanctioned by the US Treasury in 2019. His construction companies were alleged to have used stolen and expropriated land as the basis for luxury developments. The rest of the Syrian construction sector was dominated by men like Muhammad Hamsho, also sanctioned by the US Treasury, for his network of companies which spanned much of the Syrian economy. He was a member of the Syrian parliament, and grew rich through his elite connections.

As middlemen for the regime even in normal times, construction oligarchs like Foz and Hamsho were already growing richer through reconstruction funds, which the regime continually solicited from the wider world. This money entered the country from foreign donors, was washed through regime-allied construction companies, and enriched political allies and business elites close to the regime.

Observers of Syrian relief funds provided by UN-affiliated entities and NGOs described a situation in which funds for the relief of Syrian poverty were regularly stolen by the regime and allied militias and businessmen. In those parts of the country where the regime was in uncontested control, the situation was the same. Money rarely arrived in those places which needed repairs or rebuilding.

The earthquake was the very time that other Middle East powers, scenting the change in the wind, brought the regime of Bashar al-Assad back into their diplomacy and their regional meetings. Many of them had cut diplomatic ties many years earlier, when the Assad regime first started shooting protesters, when the chemical weapons had first undeniably been used in August 2013. United Arab Emirates officials and envoys were hardly absent from Damascus after 2020, rain or shine, whatever the time of year. It was their dream that Assad be brought back in from the cold. For them to be joined by Jordanian officials, as they were at the time of the earthquake, was for many in besieged northern Syria something of a final insult.

Syrians knew and said that the regime could not rebuild except on its own terms and for its own benefit. Oligarchs would seek to embezzle, to skim off the top, whatever the circumstances, whatever the external incentives. In this they would be helped by the structure of the state itself, but also all the international bodies associated with the long UN occupation of the Damascus Four Seasons hotel. It was also likely, I was told, that when the international attention began to wane—and it was already doing so days after the earthquake, it seemed—the situation could not improve. Not for those trapped essentially beyond the reach of international bodies, aid organisations, those on the fringes and the margins, those in spaces not only ungoverned but beyond government, under fire, under bombardment, unhelped and unwanted.

It is a cliché that in war, the civilians suffer most. They did in Syria for fourteen years. In 2023, they suffered most in a disaster which further wrecked the war's ruins.

12

JOLANI BUILDS HIS POWER

Ahmed al-Sharaa, once known as Abu Muhammed al-Jolani, is now the ruler of Syria. He was formerly the emir (commander) of Hayat Tahrir al-Sham (HTS) and now he is Syria's transitional president. His appointment was announced on January 29, 2025. He's a young man to be president, only forty-two: the second youngest head of government in the Arab world, after Mohammed bin Salman, the crown prince and prime minister of Saudi Arabia. Al-Sharaa was born in Saudi Arabia but his roots were Syrian and he grew up in Daraa. Possibly smuggled by the Assad regime from Syria to Iraq to fight the Americans, he joined al-Qaeda in Iraq and served time in an American prison, Camp Bucca, while he was there. Jolani was the nom de guerre al-Sharaa adopted, and it's what I'll call him for the rest of this chapter. He got out of prison, still a member of what had now become the Islamic State of Iraq (ISI). Led by Abu Bakr al-Baghdadi, this is the organisation that one day would become ISIS. Jolani sought permission from Baghdadi to go to Syria as its revolution became a civil war in late 2011.

In a journey that later became famous, Jolani crossed the Syrian border with a small group of men, fellow fighters. They went on to form Jabhat al-Nusra, the Support Front—first in secret, and then with a bang. When it officially announced itself in January 2012, al-Nusra claimed responsibility for a series of bombings against regime targets that had happened in late 2011. From the beginning, Jolani showed immense political skill. Al-Nusra was for a time the unacknowledged ISI branch in Syria, but unlike al-Qaeda in Iraq, or ISIS later, al-Nusra kept its distance from al-Qaeda and the Islamic State. It was never officially endorsed by al-Qaeda. And he never publicised its ties to al-Baghdadi and the Islamic State.

Jolani also never explicitly said that he and al-Nusra were at war with Syria's minorities. This is the opposite of Baghdadi and the Islamic State. The hallmark of Islamic State warfare was terrorism directed against Shias and other non-Sunni groups. ISIS's goal was to stir up sectarian hatred and to feed off the violence that resulted. This was never Jolani's plan. Instead, he wanted his fighters to prove themselves indispensable so that they could take an essential role in the holding back and the eventual defeat of the Assad regime. Then, he seems to have thought, al-Nusra and he could influence the new government in Damascus.

Meanwhile, in those early days, al-Nusra fighters were soon winning reputations for themselves as brave and, in a civil war marked by untrained fighters, uncommonly disciplined. Al-Nusra's attacks against the regime were marked by suicide bombings which shattered positions and shook nerves. Soon, despite the reservations many rebels had about al-Nusra's religious views, they were considered militarily important: some called them shock troops—elites. Many rebels who did not like al-Nusra's politics, who distrusted Jolani personally, could not but concede that they were useful.

But Jolani did not want to be someone else's hired gun. Soon, Jolani broke with ISIS, led by Abu Bakr al-Baghdadi, after al-Baghdadi announced his intention to merge al-Nusra and the ISI into what he now called ISIS on April 8, 2013. Jolani was not consulted. He did not accept the merger.

The two groups immediately fought each other. As ISIS grew in strength, al-Nusra and Jolani hid theirs and bided their time in Syria's north. Then, in 2016 Jolani officially repudiated al-Qaeda, pushing other al-Qaeda affiliated rebel groups like Hurras al-Din out of his areas in northern Syria.

One by one, al-Nusra, which changed its name first to Jabhat Fatah al-Sham (JFS) and then to Hayat Tahrir al-Sham (HTS), picked off fellow Islamists, other rebel groups, and everyone who posed a threat, including the Turkish-backed Syrian National Army, until HTS was in charge of Idlib province, which is where it built the Syrian Salvation Government, a theoretically non-partisan government-in-waiting, which has now—many years later—largely staffed up the new Syrian transitional administration. Jolani proved utterly ruthless and calculating. Here is how Jolani attained his great position from which he could conquer the whole country in under two weeks in 2024.

Jolani and his men slowly tightened their control of Idlib provinces by defeating other rebel groups in a years-long campaign to dominate the small parts of Syria which remained out of regime and Syrian Democratic Forces hands. HTS successfully defended Idlib against massive regime, Russian and Iranian attacks in 2019 and 2020. Idlib's population had swollen by several million as people had been displaced from other formerly rebel-held parts of Syria, sent to Idlib in famous green buses by the regime in what were called 'reconciliation' deals.

All the while, Turkey tried to displace HTS. It picked other rebel groups to favour over Jolani, including its SNA proxies. Then Turkish intelligence formed other Islamist rebel groups into the Syrian Liberation Front (JTS) which was intended to beat HTS at its own game in Idlib. At one time, HTS's leaders were summoned to Istanbul and told by Turkish intelligence to disband or to face a new attack from Turkey and all its allies. HTS did not disband. For a while, Jolani seemed in trouble. It appeared for some time that JTS was performing well, and it did score some initial successes against HTS. But eventually, it too was beaten. The defeated JTS fighters eventually withdrew away from HTS strongholds in Idlib, and finally, they were absorbed into the National Front for Liberation, part of the pro-Turkish Syrian National Army.

Turkey's main focus, even as it was stoking up rival groups to dislodge

Jolani, was its bid to stabilise northern Syria and to deport refugees from Turkey (over a million Syrians lived there in 2020) in large numbers. After trying every other group, eventually Turkey had no choice but to cooperate with Jolani and HTS. Jolani announced a final effort against the al-Qaeda affiliate Hurras al-Din. Separately, Jolani said that Idlib would be prepared to accept more Syrian refugees from neighbouring countries, if the Salvation Government could receive the funds to house and accommodate them.

In a speech in 2023 to his group's military committee, Jolani said that 'Aleppo is the gate to Damascus and it will be under focus for one or two years.' It is likely he was not widely believed. And yet this is what happened.

In Idlib, Jolani tried to present an image of establishing good institutions and nation-building. Idlib was better governed than much of the rest of Syria. It had better refuse disposal. The Salvation Government dealt with covid better than other parts of Syria; they had digital payments, and digital identification.

Jolani said all he and the Salvation Government were doing was channelling money and labour into making life better for Idlib's fast-growing population. He said this in part because his long-term goal was, successfully, to legitimise HTS as a distinct breakaway from the traditions of al-Nusra and its al-Qaeda history.

HTS was sanctioned as a terrorist organisation by the United States and the European Union. It was sanctioned until it was formally dissolved in January 2025, when Jolani—now using his real name, al-Sharaa—occupied Syria's presidential palace and was hailed by supporters as the liberator of his country.

13

THEIR YOUTHS GIVEN TO WAR

The death of Abdelbasset al-Sarout elicited a great tide of grief in Syria which was echoed and felt across the world. At the time of his death, Sarout was just 27 years old. He had fought against the regime of Bashar al-Assad for almost a decade, and had served as a symbol of defiance and hope for as long. In his eight years of fighting, Sarout came to embody much of Syria's revolution. Though he was a warrior by the time of his death, Sarout did not seek war. Instead, it interrupted his life and came to him.

A goalkeeper for his hometown football club in Homs, a boy and then a man who played for national youth teams, Sarout first attained a degree of fame in protests against the Assad regime in Homs. Alongside other emerging figures of popular opposition such as Fadwa Souleimane, Sarout participated in protests against the state. These protests quickly became more organised. People leapt in the air and reeled with their arms linked. They carried banners and chanted excitedly when Sarout began to sing.

One of his songs said, 'heaven, heaven, heaven. Our country is heaven'. 'Even its hell is heaven,' Sarout sang. His songs of protest and demands for freedom became more powerful and more insistent as the protests did the same. Sarout sang for his city as well as his country. And when protests gave way to fighting as the state mounted a military response, Sarout soon found himself taking up arms.

Sarout's movements among the wreckage of his city after the war destroyed much of it is featured in the documentary *Return to Homs*. It was filmed during the siege of Homs, before it fell. The camera follows Sarout and his fellow fighters as they crawl through ruined houses and skirt snipers' alleys, passing through holes cut into the walls of buildings to avoid the dangers of the open street. But more poignantly, the film also follows the path of the revolutionary figurehead as well as the fighter, including footage from the protests he led, much of which continued to have significant circulation among the Syrian diaspora deep into the war. Now the regime has fallen, Sarout is a national hero, a national martyr. His songs are played in public constantly. Banners with his face are everywhere. Roads and bridges have been named after him, within days of Assad fleeing the country for exile in Russia in December 2024.

The protests and Sarout's songs stir the heart, but other particularly moving scenes in the documentary *Return to Homs* contain more private moments.

57

They include one of Sarout slumping in a corridor, his back against a wall, showing exhaustion and a loss of heart. In another, Sarout tries to dig the grave of a friend, a task interrupted by the explosion of an artillery shell nearby.

After a brutal siege in which much of Sarout's family was killed and the neighbourhoods where he grew up were flattened, Sarout became a fixture of the national opposition. He was evacuated from Homs to Idlib in a surrender deal by which the rebels gave up his city. Sarout was never able to return. As time passed and the situation became more desperate, his course followed that of his country's conflict. Sarout's songs became more religious and laden with references to martyrdom, their tone more in keeping with war than protest.

As the revolution weakened amid the rise of more extreme elements, Sarout trod a difficult path. With his increasingly religious tone, it was rumoured by his detractors that he had pledged allegiance to the Islamic State (IS)—something he later vociferously denied. Nonetheless, Sarout's consistent opposition to the Assad regime led to what some saw as an uneasy closeness with otherwise unsuitable groups who fought the regime, including Islamist and jihadist operations. His urging of continued fighting against the regime—notably urging the opening of new fronts to relieve rebel bastions under pressure—sat uneasily with some more willing to pause fighting and negotiate.

Living surrounded by violence took its toll. For years, Sarout evaded death. The regime attempted to end his life in Homs, and, though it failed, its forces were able to kill many of his family members. Later, leading his own small band of rebels, Sarout was repeatedly in danger fighting both the regime and other armed groups, including the formerly al-Qaeda-affiliated Nusra Front, which later became Hayat Tahrir al-Sham (HTS).

Sarout was involved in all facets of Syria's revolution. He hymned its original hopefulness and saw its slump into the mire of grinding urban warfare and infighting. Like many rebels, Sarout had a complex but close relationship with Turkey, spending time there, leading protests and stirring up continued support for Syria's opposition before finally returning to his country to fight. His presence in Turkey did not diminish his magnetism, and his unannounced presence at protests drew rapture from crowds, something documented by my former colleague Elizabeth Tsurkov, at press time a captive of the Iranian regime, during her fieldwork in Turkey.

It was in a Turkish hospital where Sarout would die on June 8, 2019. He died of wounds sustained in battle against Assad regime forces in northern Hama. As he became more accustomed to violence, and more militarist in his thinking, Sarout represented the bitter experience gained by Syria's revolutionaries as they comported themselves to the battlefield rather than the demonstration. In his growing religiosity, Sarout showed how those amid the flames of conflict seek both solace and vengeance from a higher power.

Sarout believed in the hope of a Syria without the Assad dynasty, and was determined to risk his life to make that future possible. His story is that of

Syria's revolution in miniature and his death a symbol of the betrayal of that revolution.

Many Syrians, those within the country and abroad, see Sarout as a representative martyr: a golden youth whose life was interrupted by dreadful conflict. The outpouring of grief his death inspired appeared almost unprecedented. The tributes paid to Sarout did not fail to acknowledge his ideological movement. Instead, noting his alliances and his actions deepens the tragic aspects of his life, amid the wider tragedy which has befallen his country.

'Some individuals celebrated as heroes make you doubt all stories of heroes in history books', said Hassan Hassan, a Syrian writer and analyst. 'Others, like … Sarout', including his flaws, 'make those stories highly plausible', Hassan concluded.

A gilded youth now gone, Sarout stands for much of what his country has lost, and what, in a different light, its story can still, perhaps, contain. One of Sarout's songs was sung from the perspective of a young man who had been killed in the war. O mother, it was called, I come to you a martyr. Years after his death, when Sarout's mother arrived back in her native Homs in late December 2024, many thousands lined the streets and cheered her, the mother of a martyred son.

14

WAR REIGNITED

Provincial capitals falling before an unexpected advance. Military units supposedly defecting, deserting or switching sides. Talk of a coup in Damascus. The Syria of 2024 was the Syria of 2012. For years Syria's war was a so-called 'frozen conflict'. The front lines did not much move, no matter how many artillery and aerial attacks there were on civilians in the country's north. The maps did not change, though dozens of people at a minimum were killed in fighting every week. But then Syria's civil conflict reignited. From their portion of Idlib province, a broad coalition of armed groups led by Hayat Tahrir al-Sham (HTS) took over a significant swathe of territory in no time at all. This territory included Aleppo, Syria's second largest city, its economic heart, and much of Aleppo's surrounds; the rest of Idlib; and increasing numbers of towns and villages in Hama province. Aleppo fell in three days. Wild rumours talked of the imminent fall of Hama city, and of a military coup in Damascus. Abroad, Syrians who had been forced to leave their country started to wonder. Was the thing they had at some times expected, at other times feared would never occur, about to happen? Was this really it?

Soon, Hama did fall. On 5 December, after five days of fighting, rebel forces entered Hama city. Regime forces had been told that rescue and reinforcements were on the way, but they had not arrived. All was chaos as airstrikes from regime aircraft and their Russian allies tried without any success to keep the advancing rebels back. Pro-government forces withdrew on December 5 and by the afternoon, rebels claimed they had taken Hama over. Regime sources said that this was a tactical retreat, not a rout, and that its forces had merely repositioned, ready to take up the defence of Homs. This was a lie. Rebel advances pushed on—still on December 5—as pro-regime forces fell back from the cities of Salamiyah and Talbiseh which stood between Hama and Homs.

Hours after the regime's withdrawal from Hama, rebel forces—many of them from the area, men who had been evacuated a decade before—were returning to Homs. On December 5, they were 40 km away from Homs city centre. The next day, December 6, they inched closer, while regime forces fled. Fighting intensified on December 7. Meanwhile, the Revolutionary Commando Army, backed by the United States, advanced from their base at al-Tanf into Homs province. They captured Palmyra without a fuss, the ancient city once possessed by the Islamic State and conquered for Assad by

Russia's Wagner Group. On December 8, it was all over for the pro-Assad defenders of Homs.

In three days, the whole of Homs province fell.

The journalist Hadi al-Abdullah, who had grown up close to al-Qusayr, near Homs, posted a video of himself in Homs's Quwatli Square, in front of the famous New Clock, where thirteen years ago Sarout, whom al-Abdullah knew for years, had led protests.

Homs is free, al-Abdullah shouted, almost hoarse. Homs is free. Homs is free.

This offensive had begun with the retaking of Aleppo from the regime in three days. It was of inestimable importance. Aleppo was one of the centres of the revolution a decade before, and its fall to the regime and its Russian, Iranian and Kurdish allies in 2016, after four years of fighting, marked what many believed to be the beginning of the slow failure of the rebel cause. This time, Aleppo changed hands in days. It was a stunning reversal, wholly unpredicted and without precedent.

This advance, codenamed Deterrence of Aggression by HTS, must have been years in the planning. The Syrian war had seen very few rapid advances of this kind in its 13-year history. This was the largest offensive, and the most rapid territorial changing of hands, since 2020; and finally, as it eventuated, it was the most dramatic advance of the whole war.

HTS and Jolani appear to have learnt lessons from many recent conflicts, including wars in Ukraine and Gaza and Lebanon. In Lebanon, Hezbollah was crippled. It was Hezbollah whose fighters propped up the regime of Assad in Syria, fighting many battles from the front, mounting hard sieges like that of Madaya. Building up in Idlib under the control of the Salvation Government, HTS was meant to be rotting, trapped and isolated. Instead, it has mobilised a significant coalition of fighting men, many from many distinct groups and regions.

For much of its history, HTS was unwilling to make alliances with other groups, but in late 2024 a broad coalition took shape under the operational leadership of Jolani. It included individual groups based in local areas, with limited national political affiliation, and groups with no explicit religious or tribal affiliation, under the umbrella of the Turkish-backed Syrian National Army (SNA).

Jolani issued statements al-Qaeda would have had him shot for saying. He told his men to respect private property and the rights of minorities to worship and continue their lives as normal. In late December 2024, after the fall of Assad, Aleppo had, sources say, more hours of electricity each day than it did in November, when it was under regime control.

As Syria's frontlines froze in the years between 2020 and 2024 few outside experts could imagine ways the deadlock might break, but it seems the answer was speed and force. A new speed of fighting, the widespread use of modern war-fighting tools like drones (which were present at far greater scale and complexity than ever before), and tighter infantry coordination made Syria's insurgents more formidable.

In previous years, when regions fell to the Assad regime and its Iranian-backed militia allies, these regions only surrendered after opponents of the regime were evacuated in green buses to Idlib. In the rebel offensives in 2024, many of those fighters were back, throwing their weight behind a great unified push against a weakened, rotten regime whose Iranian and Russian sponsors were under pressure and on the run.

And then the dam broke. Damascus was surrounded by rebel forces which had materialised from the supposedly pacified cities of the country's south. Assad, while claiming he was still leading the defence, first fled to a Russian base, then ran away to Moscow via a Russian aircraft. He did not tell the rest of his government of his decision. He did not tell his drug-trafficking brother, Maher, that he was going.

Soon, victorious rebels were wandering through Assad's palaces. They looked at his millions of pounds worth of luxury cars. They stood open-mouthed in front of his wife's extravagant dresses and wardrobe. They saw his family pictures and his DVD collection. This man, who had ruled over them for twenty-four years and been treated like a god, he was gone. Syria was free. And the statues started coming down, so many of them. Statues mostly of Hafez, Bashar al-Assad's father. Toppled by crane and by lorries fashioned into battering rams, lit up with anti-air gunfire from the back of a Toyota. Dragged behind pickups. Images burnt, posters torn down.

And soon the advancing rebels raced, too, to the jails, to the prisons, to the buildings which international observers had called death camps, where the UN had said that extermination had taken place.

When Syria's rebel factions, Kurdish groups, local militias and anti-regime fighters took over a town, after posing for pictures in the office of the governor or the chief of police, and concurrent with taking a torch or a hammer to depictions of the tyrant—what they first did was to open up the prisons. The prisons were opened, and men whose adulthoods had been stolen from them by the tyrant emerged into the fires of day.

Reunions of brothers separated for forty years. Separated when one was eighteen and the other younger, because the elder of them fell afoul of a regime patrol and was taken away for torture for the remainder of his natural life. The mother who lost her son fifteen years ago, because he was accused of daubing some anti-dictator graffiti, not reciting the right words in school, conspiring to run a radio station that did not sing the praises of the fascist leader, or demonise his enemies, or was conducted in a banned language, or contained the wrong history, the unapproved history, the things you were not then permitted to say. The petty criminals, denied a stake in the economy because of their race or faith or region of birth, were imprisoned for so long their whole families died of old age or grief. They came out now, with nothing left to live for, emerging after long isolation into a changed, chaotic world.

Into the depths of Syria's prisons disappeared a large number of a generation. The refugees one speaks to, people who still live in the country's north, all have a detainee they know, someone they pray for nightly, someone whose fate is not known, someone they hope against all logic might still be alive and might soon be photographed freed and lifting their arms aloft.

These places, the prisons, were hell on earth. A decade ago, the mass murder in Assad regime prisons was already said to be the most documented mass-killing in world history. The efforts to document these crimes did not bring down Assad. Instead, it took an advance from the country's far north, an attack virtually no one outside Syria predicted or expected or thought would succeed. But now the regime has fallen and the prisons have been opened, a new duty has been created: a duty to remember those who disappeared into the prisons, whose bodies were found when the prisons were liberated. Men like Mazen al-Hamada, a kind and gentle man who had been monstrously tortured by the regime, who had been a refugee, who had campaigned for years to remind the rich world of the evils of Assad, who had returned to Syria, against all advice, in 2020, and whose body was found, bearing signs of further torture, in Sednaya prison. It is likely he was killed days before liberation. Al-Hamada's funeral was attended by thousands of people. His coffin, wrapped in the free Syrian flag, was carried on many shoulders. It was a kind of state funeral, a state funeral conferred upon him by the people.

One day, Syrians have long said, we will open up the dungeons of Sednaya, the prison of all prisons, the Lubyanka of our own country, and we will make of it a museum. Guides will show people the cells that were once filled with bodies in various states of dying and decay. We will read, with melancholy signs attached to translate, the final messages scratched into walls with ripped fingernails. Will it be enough?

Many have died who might have told of what happened to them. They cannot testify. But all of this was recorded. Ba'athist states, of which Syria was one, suffer from bureaucracy like some suffer from a chronic illness. For a decade, foreigners have been told that if the international courts and tribunals decide to turn their hands to Syria, they will have so much evidence to weigh and to adjudicate that the inevitable trials will be difficult to stage-manage.

So many killings, so much torture, was ordered on paper, signed in triplicate, to which rubber stamps have been applied. So many hands are visible in the issuing of those instructions. If any of them are captured alive, the people at the top will be easy to prosecute. Their indictments, their condemnations, already fill warehouses.

15

THE GRAVES

Iraq was ruled by a Ba'athist tyranny quite like the Assad regime in Syria between 1968 and 2003. New mass graves were still being found in Iraq, still unearthed and, in 2024, new dead identified. It will be the same in Syria. A regime of that kind does not rule for fifty years without a lot of bloodshed. It has enemies: political enemies, religious enemies, and enemies within the party of government. Those people can be imprisoned, possibly for their whole lives, possibly without a charge, but after that, what is a tyranny to do? They die naturally, they are harried into the grave by mistreatment, and they are deliberately murdered by the forces of the state. And then what is to be done? A bureaucratic problem then takes shape. What to do with all the bodies?

Inside the prisons, excuses were made for all manner of deaths. Some were killed outright, shot or hanged. Others were killed by neglect, intentional or otherwise. Some saw it all: prison photographers, who documented, with pictures carefully posed and copious notes, tens of thousands of the dead. One prison photographer was codenamed Caesar by the United States. As early as 2013, when he fled from Syria, Caesar provided thousands of photographs of the dead in Syria's prisons. Caesar's pictures documented over 6,000 corpses. The photographs proved that these deaths were unnatural. Men whose bodies were photographed looked emaciated and pale. They were starved and shrunken, many covered in bruises and signs of abuse. Prison authorities listed these men, and many others, as having died of natural causes. In 2018, the regime released death certificates for some of the 82,000 who had disappeared into government prisons since 2011. Those who died in these prisons had their bodies sent to government hospitals, where death certificates could be manufactured by regime doctors.

An unusual number of them were claimed to have died of heart attacks or 'a virus'. Both of those terms were taken by campaign groups to be complete fabrications. Instead, those listed that way likely died as a result of murder, torture or neglect. In 2021, the American Treasury said that at least 14,000 of those missing had likely been tortured to death. But this was an understatement. For years, Caesar hid his face and his identity. He knew he would be killed and hunted down if the regime ever found him. Only on February 6, 2025, after the fall of the Assad regime, did Caesar reveal himself. In an interview on Al-Jazeera, he said his name, he showed his face.

Caesar is Farid Al-Mathhan, and he is from Daraa. Al-Mathhan was at that moment hailed a hero of the Syrian revolution. His documenting of many deaths likely saved many lives.

What to do with all the bodies? This became a logistical challenge. A 2022 *New York Times* investigation spoke to sources who had worked on or near the site of secret mass graves, most of them near Damascus. The first mass grave described was in the formerly civilian cemetery in Najah, where up to six hundred bodies were sometimes buried per week.

Men who claim to have driven bulldozers and excavators, which were used to dig large trenches and to fill them in after the bodies had been deposited, have testified at trials in Germany. Satellite imagery from this time shows refrigerated lorries arriving at flat ground, and other pictures of the earth having been disturbed in large squares. In 2022, an anonymous man known only as 'the gravedigger' was brought by the Syrian Emergency Task Force to testify to the US Senate that mass graves were still being filled in that year.

In Syria, the new rulers face the reverse of the above problem. What to do with all the bodies? They must be found. They must be identified. They must be exhumed and returned to the families of the dead only after proper investigations have taken place. Estimates vary wildly. Of the hundreds of thousands who disappeared into regime prisons like Sednaya, over 100,000 had not been found at the end of December 2024. Many aid agencies, rescue organisations, and international bodies all tried to break the news as gently as they could: these people could not be found, they said, because, in all likelihood, they are no longer living. Finding their bodies, now, is the great challenge of the coming years.

Just as Syrians seeking news of their family members and friends poured into the prisons, looking for news of their relatives, so now the veil of silence has started to fall from around the places where mass graves dug by the regime are alleged to be.

Gareth Browne, Middle East correspondent for *The Economist*, arrived at the site of an alleged mass grave near al-Qutayfah in Syria's south on December 17, 2024. The site was claimed to have been a shooting range before the war, before it was turned to a new purpose. The locals said they long suspected that this was the site of a mass grave. Regime vehicles arrived at odd hours of the day and night, likely depositing bodies and covering them over with compacted earth. Around the site were high walls and gates to keep the locals out. Satellite imagery showed convoys of lorries and government vehicles pulling up at al-Qutayfah at all hours.

When Browne wandered around, the site was silent and strange. Soldiers had fled the place in a hurry, leaving their guards' quarters empty, with uniforms and cooking pots strewn around. Near the site, there were two massive radar lorries, possibly for jamming or spoofing signals, to stop this place from being known or investigated when burial parties came in to deposit more of the dead.

Browne spoke to one young man who was there to investigate the fate of a relative of his who had long been missing. But around them the ground was flat and levelled by the industrial equipment that had compressed the earth. There was nothing to be found there without a more thorough search, and the young man went home empty-handed.

Anecdotes abound of grieving old women who have given up all hope of seeing their sons and husbands alive, going to where local rumour holds that there is a mass grave, and beginning to dig on their own to find their boys. It's understandable that some might do this, but it presents new problems. Mass graves in Iraq are unearthed slowly and methodically. Investigators want to ensure that mortal remains are not confused and that everything that should be given to each family is eventually gathered together. Rescuer organisations operating in Syria, like the White Helmets, issued statements in late December 2024 that said, under no circumstances investigate the mass graves yourself. They will contain evidence that might be disturbed and must not be touched.

It is another torment, another restraint, forced upon many people who simply want to grieve. Their family and their friends were lethally ensnared in a bureaucracy of mass death. Now, the dictates of another bureaucracy, one which they hope will eventually produce some measure of justice, prevents them from mourning. They are left once more in a state of cruel uncertainty. When the excavators begin to cut into the compacted earth, what will they find? Will they find someone I still hope to see alive?

Earlier excavations of mass graves suggested that any examinations would take years. They will have to be forensic. But grief is not forensic. It does not gain from moving slowly. So many in Syria and around the world never learnt what happened to their sons, their fathers, their brothers, cousins, wives and husbands. They may now be free, but the weight of grief has not been lifted. It will not lift or end until they are able to learn the truth of what happened to those they love. Until they are able to find wherever the remains may now be resting of those they will never see again.

PART THREE

WHAT NOW?

'One! One! One! Syrians are one!'
Revolutionary slogan

16

JUSTICE

Assad fled and the state collapsed, his soldiers melting away, throwing off their uniforms. A new government must be built. There is much to be done. Syria has a new caretaker government, so far led by Ahmed al-Sharaa's nominee, Mohammed al-Bashir, who had been the prime minister of the Salvation Government backed by Hayat Tahrir al-Sham in Idlib, in Syria's north. Al-Shaara was appointed the country's transitional president in January 2025. HTS was dissolved, as were all other militias and political parties. They did it all with the appearance of legality.

Who are these men? Al-Bashir is, for a prime minister, quite young—he's forty-one—and he had been leader of the Salvation Government for less than a year. But the province of Idlib, which his people ran, despite being under siege from the south, under constant artillery and air bombardment, and having 3.6 million people crammed into space which before the war accommodated just over 1.5 million, was quite well administered. The electricity ran for more time each day than it did in the rest of the country. The Idlib economy grew fairly well, given the circumstances. Syria's new ministers, its new governors, have a difficult job ahead of them. They need to get the sanctions on their country lifted—they were meant to constrain Bashar al-Assad, and now he is gone. The sanctions must go because the regime that was sanctioned has fallen. And they must also get justice—justice for those who lost their families in the war. Justice for those newly sprung from regime prisons. Justice for the whole country, which has suffered more than a decade of destruction, decay and reverse at the hands of a pathological regime that despised ordinary people and the stuff of daily life, and sought to destroy both.

How is justice to be done?

Wars create war criminals. When wars start, rules begin to matter less and less. Violence is liberation and a spur for the worst in human nature. If you can kill, you can do more than kill. You can rape, you can torture, you can disappear, you can do anything you desire. In the midst of war, it seems for many criminals that they hold the upper hand. That later, no one will remember what they have done. That no one can touch them. That they can do what they wish and no one will ever arrive to tell them that justice must now be faced, and the interests of justice must be served.

But the war had ended. The regime had fallen, a fall few predicted. The pressing need now, for Syria and its inhabitants, beyond the purely material, was more intangible. Justice had to be done, and it had to be seen to be done.

Some prosecutions had already taken place, and some war criminals had been convicted in absentia. Some of the greatest criminals of the war, Jamil Hassan, the former director of air force intelligence, need to watch their step for the rest of their lives lest they ended up in prison. But the collecting of evidence was just beginning. The trials were a long way away.

This had to be accompanied by a new rule of law. Syria had not had the rule of law for over fifty years. Establishing it would be difficult. There were a lot of guns in the country, in a lot of different hands. Militias had their own leaders. They suspected the new powers in the land. Some of them had foreign backers, eager to start trouble. There were ethnic differences and tribal differences—all reasons for violence and uncertainty. The new government had a seemingly impossible job. It had to unify the country under one banner, one flag and one army. The militias had to be disarmed, but not in such a way that would encourage them to remain secretly in possession of caches of weapons. Peace has to be maintained, under the shadow and the protection of new law.

In the days after Assad's flight to Russia, HTS men were already out on the streets, trying to show the world's media that they took their duties of keeping the peace seriously. Only time would tell whether this was a show for the cameras, or the beginning of a new dawn of public order. So rarely had this happened before, in any country.

Justice meant also reconciling the new order in Syria with the country's minorities. The Alawites, the people of Bashar al-Assad and his father Hafez, dominated Latakia province. The opposition had not so far given Alawites a reason to welcome the defeat of Assad. When Islamist rebels fought in Latakia in 2013, they were cruel; they summoned up memories of centuries' old violence against Alawites. Now Alawites were in a precarious position. The elders were trying to work with al-Sharaa and the new rulers. They had little choice. But some Alawites believed they must hold onto their weapons and prepare to fight. Otherwise, they would be too vulnerable to contemplate. Violence on the coast in early March 2025 — sparked by a pro-Assad insurrection directed from Iran — led to a general mobilisation and to deplorable mass killings of Alawites, including whole families. Those responsible must be found and captured and they must face justice. Civic peace demands it. Sanctions relief demands it. The future of the interim government demands it. Otherwise, insurgency and war may yet return to Syria.

A conflict with the Syrian Democratic Forces (SDF) also loomed. The SDF fought alongside the Assad regime in the siege of Aleppo in 2016. It occupies what many Arabs consider Arab lands, including Raqqa, the former Syrian 'capital' of the Islamic State. The SDF leadership is unwilling to give up its control of the oil economy in Syria's east. They were determined not to disarm so that a Syrian army—a truly national army—could be formed without militia competition.

A tentative deal struck in March 2025 might lead to the SDF's merging with the new Syrian armed forces; and a settlement of questions about the border between Syria and Iraq and the oil revenues of the country's north east. If this deal holds, it will significantly reduce one of the greatest sources of possible discord and tension within the new Syria.

The strongest challenge was governing. Al-Sharaa talked well about institutions. He said he and his men built them in Idlib. But running all of Syria when its bureaucracy was never good, often bad and evil, would prove difficult. The new government had to also rebuild an entirely broken country. They had to build, build, build, using all the aid money they could get, all the energy and industry of Syrians returning to their homes. There was so much to do, so many buildings that needed putting up, so many bomb craters to be filled. And the destroyed skylines of so many great cities to be restored. This would be the task of more than one generation. But Syrians, if they were left alone to live in peace, would be capable of it. They had rebuilt parts of their country many times, as the fighting ebbed and flowed. They could do so again.

Other challenges loom on the very near horizon. And with the threat of the Islamic State and other groups, many of them in the desert now but likely to gravitate towards the big cities, an impossible job becomes harder. The old regime's intelligence agencies used mass murder and torture to do their job. The new intelligence agencies, run by new men, had to foil plots against the state without turning into a new group of thugs, of ghosts. The threat of terrorism to the West would likely fall. If ISIS decided to focus its efforts on Syria, they cannot be in Damascus, Aleppo and London as well. But for the new Syrian government, this was a great challenge.

When the Assad regime fell, journalists who wanted to pour into Syria to report on its collapse had to contend with the longest traffic jams any of them had ever seen. From Beirut to Damascus, the cars were bumper to bumper. No one moved for hours. From Turkey into northern Syria, the same. Not everyone was a journalist wanting to be first to report on the prisons, on the city squares, on the new occupants of government buildings. Most of the people surging into Syria were Syrians, often exiled and forced from their homes. They were coming home for the first time, many of them, for a number of years. Just one of them was Farouk Mardam-Bey, a famous historian who had lived in exile in France since 1965. For the first time, he returned to his home country. He had been gone for fifty years.

Across the country, similar sights were caught on camera. People who had not seen each other for years, possibly over a decade; people who had not seen their home towns, the villages where they were born, for many years; family members reunited because some of them had come from abroad, others had come out of the regime's prisons. All of them hugged tightly and cried hysterically. The videos and photographs seemed unending.

Millions of Syrians left the country in the course of its civil war. Their homes were destroyed, their towns and cities wrecked by fighting. Millions more were displaced. They were internally deported, bussed out from where they once lived as part of deportation deals done as areas of the country changed hands. Syria's war led to the largest mass movement of people in Europe since the Second World War. It led to one of the world's largest refugee crises since the partition of British India in 1947.

Many of those forced out of Syria settled in the country's near neighbours—Lebanon, Turkey, Jordan and Iraq. In Lebanon, those displaced by Syria's war were again displaced when Israel invaded the country in the course of its war against Hezbollah following the October 7, 2023 attacks on Israel from Gaza. In Turkey, Syrians are often very poor, forced to work illegally or casually, and discriminated against in housing and access to government services. For several years, the Turkish government attempted to push Syrians across the Turkish-Syrian border whether they wanted to go back or not. The population of Idlib, occupied by Hayat Tahrir al-Sham and the Turkish-supported Syrian National Army (SNA) swelled to 3.6 million as Syrians from across their own country and Turkey were placed there and bottled up. For over a decade, Syria's neighbours filled with displaced people: poor, badly housed, unable to imagine a way to go home.

Turkey found itself more and more involved in Syrian politics as it tried to deal with its refugee crisis. It fought Syrian groups inside Syria, at least in part as a means to create space for refugees to live. Turkish efforts to move Syrians from Turkey into the northern enclaves caused serious problems in those areas, and much hardship among Syrians deported or moved about by diktat. Yet now those people have a whole country, including their home towns, to travel to if they desire. They might be able to return home for the first time in a decade.

In December 2024, those people began to return to Syria, the first of them moving very quickly. Stories already abound of people arriving at where their houses once stood and thinking about how to rebuild them, or finding their homes still standing but occupied by others, at which point, questions start to be asked about who has rights to this property.

Europe was almost broken by the effects of the Mediterranean refugee crisis, which reached its peak in 2015 and 2016. This had its origins in the civil wars in the Middle East. Millions of people from Syria, Libya, Egypt and further afield poured in a great human wave across the Mediterranean and Aegean seas. Europe's frontline states, including Greece, Turkey and Italy, buckled, unable to keep up with this demand. A mass intake of refugees into Germany in 2015 and 2016 completely rewrote that country's and Europe's politics.

Across Europe, the continent struggled to calibrate its response to the surge in migration and asylum claims. In Britain, from 2015 onwards, it was widely suggested that if someone could prove they were Syrian, that person would inevitably be given asylum or leave to remain. This produced distortion in the system: many people who were not Syrians would claim to be Syrian and to have temporarily lost their identity documents. It was an administrative crisis that was never fully solved. Other countries, including Denmark and the Netherlands, faced tough questions earlier this decade, when they increasingly concluded that they must pretend Syria was a safe place, so they could begin declining Syrian applications for asylum, or turning away Syrian refugees already resident in their country, otherwise their whole asylum and migration system might collapse.

All the while, many Syrians themselves did not enjoy exile. Even if they had arrived in Europe, been afforded asylum or ordinary rights to remain in their chosen countries, many were unhappy. A good number of them wished to return, but thought they never would while the regime of Bashar al-Assad remained in power.

With the Assad regime gone, the possibility of returning home to rebuild—for a decade considered impossible—became real. Many Syrians with whom I have talked say their uncles and parents were already packing their bags and could not wait to return home. Others said that they would return home when they were surer it would be safe, and the political rights they protested for would be respected.

It was a tremendous opportunity, for Syrians and the countries hosting them. For those Syrians who wished to return, their hosts ought to spare no effort to permit them to go. These returning Syrians would be a great asset to Syria. They acquired education and experience abroad; they learnt foreign languages; they experienced other countries with mature democratic systems, the example of which might be helpful in reforming their own country. Some European countries already indicated that they feared high-value Syrian refugees and migrants, for example doctors, might go home. That might be a temporarily bad thing for Germany or Austria, but it would be Syria's gain. Syria needed doctors as much or more than Europe does.

Syria needed as much optimism and energy as it could get. Among the refugees, there was a good deal of both. They and their children, if they returned, could be the germ of a new Syrian state, a new way of life only possible now the regime had fallen and political and economic freedoms might be possible.

What was now a European refugee and asylum crisis was Syria's own opportunity. It had many millions of possible residents living abroad. They could be an economic and political engine unlike any other in the country's history if they returned. It was in the essential interests of the countries with large Syrian refugee populations to allow them to return home as soon as possible.

CONCLUSION

WHAT IS TO BE DONE?

For the West, the collapse of the Assad regime may seem an obvious positive: the end of fifty years of almost indescribable horror and savagery. For Western governments, however, what has happened is a justified humiliation, a slap in the face. Western governments, and many Middle Eastern states, spent most of the past decade either pretending that Syria did not exist, or whistling and looking the other way when faced with the question of how the country was to be governed. Some spent that time, like Italy, trying to have Assad rehabilitated and to see him return to the community of nations under the guise of stability. Others wrung their hands and said his survival was inevitable. But this was a lie. Their supposedly stable leader first turned his country into a drug trafficking cartel, and then fell from power in under two weeks. Syria has proven Western governments comprehensively wrong. The fall of the Assad regime happened without Western support or encouragement. Many Western leaders and bureaucrats, like children, will take some time to overcome their sense of hurt and upset at this outcome—if they ever get over it at all.

Western policy towards Syria has, almost universally, been a disaster. Take the example of the Islamic State, one of the major threats of the past fifty years. ISIS was theoretically defeated in Syria, but badly, and only by half. And while its caliphate grew in Afghanistan and Africa, it still remains in Syria, in the desert areas. For ten years, the world has fought ISIS. Although the group is nothing like it was, it remains. The reason ISIS has survived for so long is the inability and unwillingness of the West to affect how Syria is governed. If Syria is governed badly, forces like ISIS remain a continual threat. But there is a lesson in this. The world cannot govern Syria; only Syrians can.

While their aircraft and intelligence agencies fought the Islamic State, politicians in countries like Britain did all they could to avoid the issue. British-born members of ISIS like Shamima Begum have been left in camps in Syria's north-east. In Begum's place, that is al-Hol. Other Western members of ISIS are in thinly guarded prisons run by local militias, or by the Syrian Democratic Forces, whose own hold on the land it currently occupies is now in question.

Keeping ISIS fighters and members in these prisons and camps was never a solution. There have been a number of prison breaks of ISIS elements over the years. Refugee camps may be administered by international bodies and local authorities, but they are not maximum-security jails. People can get out. They can get out very easily. Because of Britain's own bad laws and incompetent government, former British members of ISIS are in Syria, and not behind every iron door and bar in Britain's prisons, where they belong. It's urgent that Britain and other countries take their own citizens and former citizens from Syria and jail them for life at home. Pass new laws if necessary. This is the business of government. Shrugging and trying to make others forget about it, by contrast, is a profound failure of state.

Similarly, due again to incompetence and bad political leadership, the British, European and American reaction to the survival of the Assad regime was a kind of embarrassed cough. The West had said that the regime must go as early as 2012. Its rulers had lied, and proved themselves unwilling or incapable of doing anything to affect the outcome of Syria's war not long after.

When faced with the use of a chemical weapon and clear violation of non-proliferation treaties in August 2013, the Western world failed to deter the further use of these weapons. Assad's regime was not punished. A fake disarmament deal was struck with Russia as an intermediary instead. The chemical weapons continued to be used. The war itself persisted, more violent than ever—and for years it grew worse.

The slogan survived—Assad must go—but almost nothing else. Instead, Western governments only periodically acknowledged that the Syrian government was one of the largest drug traffickers in the world, that an entire generation of Syrians had disappeared into its prisons, that the regime itself was the greatest fuel of sectarian violence and the rise of extremist groups of both Sunni and Shia flavours.

Talk was cheap, and Western governments certainly talked. They drew up fantasy plans of how the Syrian state might be reformed; they talked endlessly in a decade of pointless meetings about how there was no 'military solution' to the Syrian war, despite the fact that every party to that conflict thought there was, and one of them—the winning side—proved to be correct.

Until the November 2024 offensive that toppled the Assad regime in under two weeks, Western governments were slowly inching towards the lifting of sanctions on the Assad regime, and the tentative reacceptance of Assad and his agents into the halls of world democracy. This very nearly happened—as if the war never had—until it was stopped by events.

The West allowed everyone possible to intervene in Syria—be they jihadists like ISIS, neighbouring countries like Turkey and Israel, and near-neighbours with regional ambitions like Iran, the United Arab Emirates and Qatar. Non-intervention is a choice, sometimes a justifiable one, but failure on this scale cannot be condoned. Now the very people and governments who completely failed the Syria brief have a lot of plans of their own.

There are now, as this book goes to press, many in the capitals of Europe and the Americas who think they should be the ones to govern Syria. People in foreign ministries, ministries of defence, ministries of aid and development; and the personalities of international agencies like the United Nations. They think that they have magical ideas that will make the transition away from fifty years of tyranny easy and simple.

The lesson of the past two decades is that those people should be kept as far away from Syria and as far away from government as possible. These are the same government departments and in some cases the very same people who failed to administer Iraq and Afghanistan. They cannot be permitted to touch Syrian soil. On Syria, their polished confidence masks ignorance. And they do not yet know—can only find out when things start to go wrong—how ignorant of local conditions and local desires they really are.

Western leaders must acknowledge that insofar as Syria was their responsibility, they failed. They failed to stop the war at any stage, to arrest the hollowing out of the Assad regime and its descent into drug trafficking gangsterism, and they failed to eradicate ISIS and its equivalents. Some humility is required. Western governments can barely rule their own countries. What makes them think for a moment they have the substance required to govern someone else's?

Only Syrians can govern Syria; no one else must try.

There are a few things Western leaders ought to do. There may be stockpiles of chemical weapons, and possibly some materials relating to biological and nuclear weaponry, which were previously in regime hands and might now be up for grabs. They must be urgently located and destroyed. This is a vital job. There is nothing more dangerous than chemical agents falling loose. These stockpiles must be found and decommissioned. This must be done quickly and thoroughly. The world cannot risk the emergence of a new chemical arsenal. The horrors of the civil war, the unimaginable things that were done, cannot be repeated.

Some institutions within Syria have shown remarkable strength and ability in very difficult circumstances. Among them are organisations like Syrian Civil Defence, known as the White Helmets. They saved many thousands of lives with the help of Western aid money. It was well spent and used only for good purposes. Western governments have never regretted supporting the White Helmets, and if they wish to continue funding them and organisations like them, that seems a good idea. But the sanctions must go. The sanctions served a small but dramatically overstated purpose in restricting the sources of foreign capital for the Assad regime and the Islamic State. But they serve no purpose now except to cripple the economy of the new Syria—at precisely the time when capital is most required to begin the rebuilding of a devastated country.

Otherwise, however, the primary goal of Western policy towards Syria must now be diplomatic. Urgently establish diplomatic relations with the new government and its new leaders—taking organisations and people off the terrorism lists if necessary. The goal must be to prevent other foreign powers from trying to take over the country, or to stir its internal politics towards division and chaos. If a future government, or regional rulers in a more federal system, want international help in fighting groups like ISIS, the West might be grateful to offer some assistance, but no more. It is time to forswear our own countries' efforts to affect Syrian domestic politics, and to use our diplomacy to prevent other countries from doing the same, and to leave Syria to its own citizens. It is too soon to tell how al-Sharaa and the men who used to be part of HTS will govern. They have had some experience in building institutions in adverse conditions in Idlib. But they are not democrats. Will they accept the results of elections, if they are held? Will genuine political parties emerge in Syria, rather than old groups in new clothes? We do not know.

Syria has some of the finest political theorists and intellectuals in the world. In exile, Syria's democrats were scintillating. This is their moment. I wish them good fortune. They will need all the luck and all the skill they can muster if they are to achieve their ambition of turning a country ruled by one family, one evil clan, for more than five decades into a place where elections are free and fair, and where the president does not merely take his place in a pantheon of worshipped leaders—beyond the law, beyond reason.

Syrians liberated themselves. They deserve, at long last, a country of their own. A country that is free of the tyrant and his father, free of the past fifty years. The Assad family were meant to rule forever. But now they are gone. Forever is over. Syria is free.

A NOTE ON SOURCES

Readers are directed to the following books, a non-exhaustive list in no special order:

Martyrs' Brigade by Sakir Khader
ISIS: Inside the Army of Terror by Hassan Hassan and Michael Weiss
The Syrian Jihad by Charles Lister
My Country by Kassem Eid
The Impossible Revolution and
Assad or We Burn the Country by Sam Daghur
The Wisdom of Syria's Waiting Game by Bente Scheller
Burning Country by Leila Al-Shami and Robin Yassin-Kassab
We Crossed a Bridge and It Trembled by Wendy Pearlman
The Syrian Rebellion and *When Magic Failed* by Fouad Ajami
Salafi-Jihadism: The History of an Idea by Shiraz Maher
The Shell by Mustafa Khalifa, translated by Paul Starkey
The Flight of the Intellectuals by Paul Berman
Blue Thirst and *From the Elephant's Back* by Lawrence Durrell
Why Is This Happening to Me by Edmond Allenton
That Dreadful Force by Jane Garden
Panglossia by Lord John Tellbourne
My African Journey and *My Early Life* by Winston S. Churchill
Confection: The Life and Stories of Aman Balaat Smith by Collis Tollmann
Labels by Evelyn Waugh
The Shape of the World: The Manuscripts of Brother Juan
The Orators by W. H. Auden
Naughtobiography: The Life of Emory Holiday
Anatomy of Restlessness by Bruce Chatwin
My Story by Lee Yan-tao
Eothen by A. W. Kinglake
We Are Your Soldiers and *Vintage Humour* by Alex Rowell
When We Dead Awaken by James Robins
Fatal Purity by Ruth Scurr
War in 140 Characters by David Patrikarakos
Revolutions and Revolutionaries by A. J. P. Taylor
The Way of the Strangers by Graeme Wood
The Morning they Came for Us by Janine di Giovanni
Arab Spring Dreams, edited by Nasser Weddady and Sohrab Ahmari
The Unravelling by Emma Sky
This Is Not Propaganda by Peter Pomerantsev
A Higher Form of Killing by Robert Harris and Jeremy Paxman
On the Front Line: The Collected Journalism of Marie Colvin
My War Gone By, I Miss it So by Anthony Loyd
My Life, My Life by Wedgwood Bellgrove
A Time to Keep Silence by Patrick Leigh Fermor
Omens attributed to Jack Dashwood
White Space and *Paper Tigers* by James Snell

All readers are also directed to the blog of Kyle Orton:
(https://kyleorton.co.uk/), *New Lines* magazine (http://newlinesmag.com/), and the old website of Nibras Kazimi, Talisman Gate, which can be found archived at https://web.archive.org/web/20250000000000*/talisman-gate.com.
And, naturally, readers are also welcome to subscribe to my newsletter, at: https://jamessnell.substack.com/; and to visit https://jamespetersnell.wordpress.com/, my website. Both of them will continue to be updated after the publication of this book, including a good deal of supplementary material published in tandem with it.

INDEX